PROJECTS
POPES AND
PRESIDENTS

*An Inspirational Journey That Shows
How You Can Overcome Life's Obstacles
and Achieve Your Dreams*

HERBERT LANG

★

Table of Contents

★

Introduction

Within a year of retiring from my eighteen-year career as a member of the Harlem Globetrotters organization as a player and a coach, I decided it was time for me to tell my story. I decided it was time to share my story in the hopes of inspiring others through my journey. I hope the readers of my story will be motivated and inspired to never give up on their dreams or journeys no matter how difficult it may seem to be at times.

In this book, I will reflect on the first forty years of my life, and along the way, I will take you on a trip from small-town Arkansas to college and around the world with the world-famous Harlem Globetrotters. I intend to share with you personal things I have endured during life as well as the values I gained throughout my life experiences. I am a believer that it's important to treat others even better than you expect to be treated by people. Throughout the book, you will recognize the way I went about taking advantage of opportunities. You will also see how every major accomplishment in my life was the direct result of others speaking up for me and trusting I would not fail them in doing so. I was forwarded opportunities I only dreamed of growing up in Brinkley, Arkansas. A little boy who would grow up from the projects of his small town to shaking hands with governors, presidents, popes, and many powerful dignitaries around the world.

I never imagined I would have traveled to nearly ninety countries around the world and have the opportunity to be a part of the most well-traveled sports team in the world. This book will take you from as far back as I can first remember. I will discuss decisions I made along the way as well as the way I dealt with pressures, success, failures, as well as tragedy.

Over my life, I have been able to appear in many nation-wide television commercials as well as reality TV shows, notably CBS's The Amazing Race.

As a Harlem Globetrotter, my nickname was "Flight Time." I now invite you to take flight with me on a journey through life and around the world. This book is your ticket, so, buckle up and be inspired.

CHAPTER ONE

From When I Can Remember

On August 1, 1976, I was born in a relatively small hospital in Forrest City, Arkansas. I was born to eighteen-year-old Herbert Lang and seventeen-year-old Linda James. I guess you could say I was the son of young high school sweethearts. As far as I can remember, my mom and dad were never together, so any recollections of their time together I know of are those of which my mom would share with me over the course of my life. Around the time I was born, my father had already joined the United States Navy. This left my mom as a single high school mom with still some high school to finish.

One of the first things I can remember as a child is probably when I was about two years old and learning how to walk. Learning to walk for me was a little different from the average toddler. This is because I had issues with my legs. My legs were extremely bowed, so it took me a little longer than normal to learn to accomplish this feat because I would typically walk with a wobble and eventually fall down!

I was a bit like Forrest Gump. I was recommended by doctors to wear the same type of corrective leg braces that Forrest wore in the legendary movie *Forrest Gump*. I remember my braces very clearly. The leg braces had metal rods running down the side with about four brown straps running horizontally. My mom says if I spent as much time trying to walk as I did trying to remove the braces, I probably would have walked a lot sooner than I did. I was a pretty determined toddler. That determination started way back then and still burns inside me today! There were several things that happened early in my life that laid the foundation for who I am today and the person I have become. Some of these things were great, and some were not so good, but they laid the foundation for me, a young man born to teenage parents raised in a small Delta town in Arkansas.

I can remember when I was four years old walking home from the town square of my hometown of Brinkley, Arkansas. It was my sister, who was born just thirteen months after me, my newborn baby brother, my mother, and myself. For us, it was a good day of getting out and about in the town. You see, my town was the size that you could walk anywhere in town in less than an hour and travel anywhere in town within twenty minutes on bicycle.

On this particular evening, a man traveling on bike became one of the first memories of my childhood. I had no idea who this man was, and I never remember seeing him before this day. He came out of nowhere on his bike as the four us casually tried to make our way back home. For some reason, as he slowed down next to us, he began to yell and curse at my mom. I had no idea what was going on and no understanding of why this was happening. I remember immediately being afraid and crying uncontrollably. Next, he began to punch my mom anywhere he could land his fist while my mom held my infant brother in her arms. There was no way she could fight back, holding my brother, and of course my sister and I were way too small to do anything except watch helplessly in fear.

I often wonder why this is one of the first things I remember in my childhood. Why, as a child, did this instance of physical abuse have to become a staple in my mind? I can tell you it wasn't the last time I would see this man. He became a constant in my life and made it seem like hitting women was a normal thing with the regularity he would abuse her.

Even as a child, it didn't take me long to realize that what I was witnessing was not right. It was not the way things were supposed to be. Children should not have to witness these sorts of things, nor should my mom or any woman have to endure this type of abuse. For me, the foundation was cemented on this matter. I knew I would never put my hands on any female the way he did my mom. I know the feeling I had back then, and I know that I would never want any woman or child to feel what I felt in those many occasions of seeing my mom with black eyes, bloody, and battered. The image of seeing my mom with black eyes on the regular having to pile on makeup to hide the abuse from outsiders as well as family members. As I reflect back on those times, I can only seem to blame poverty and lack of adequate education.

Many people may not understand some of the hardships of growing up poor in a small town racially divided—growing up in the projects of a small town. Most of us, when we think of projects today, we think of the projects of large cities like Chicago, Detroit, and New York. Those are not the only projects that exist in America or the world. Imagine growing up as some of the poorest people in the smallest towns you can

3

imagine, as I grew up. Nothing came easily, for sure. The way I grew up made me who I am today, and if I said I would change a thing about the way I grew up, I would be lying. I'll just say growing up the way I did made me who I am, and I would not change who I have become as a result of the many hardships I faced. The hardships of being the oldest of six to a mom who had all six of us before she turned twenty-six years of age.

One of the great things about growing up in a small town like Brinkley is the sense of family. I was lucky enough to have pretty much all of my grandparents around and a part of my life from the beginning. They were always a shining light to me and a sense of relief to my siblings and me when things seemed to spin out of control. Having them always gave us an outlet to have a place to go and find solace when things weren't the best. I would say for me as the oldest even more so than my younger five siblings. You might ask, why for me more so than my younger siblings? Here is the reason.

Except for my younger three siblings, we all pretty much had different dads. My dad's parents and grandparents always took me in, filling the void of rarely never having my dad around, as after he got out of the military, he relocated to Dallas, Texas. For me, my dad's parents provided me another place to go during times of chaos. A place to go when we didn't have electricity or water in our home because we didn't have the money to pay the bills. A place to go when we didn't have any food to eat and had just made the last syrup sandwiches. This was another place I could go when I would get enough of being woken in the middle of the nights as result of the domestic abuse lashed by Greg, the man on the bike and the father of my younger three siblings.

4

I can remember so many nights my younger brother and I just smothered into the corner of the bed together, trying to ignore the yelling and abuse that happened so regularly. I cried myself to sleep so many nights, so many that I can't even remember. Nights that consisted of trembling, rapid heartbeats, sweating, and even asthma attacks.

As a child, I could never understand why my mom allowed him to stay around. In my eyes, he was the perfect example of everything a man was not supposed to be. There were only a couple of things he was passionate about. One was smoking marijuana, and the other was basketball. Growing up in my projects, we lived right next door to probably the biggest drug dealer in my hometown at the time. Greg would always send me over to buy joints for him to smoke. I remember buying many prerolled joints for a dollar each. Over the years, the prices would go up, but I was a regular joint purchaser for him.

He never worked, so the way he would get money is steal from my mom or load all six of us kids into the car to go to the store with a food stamp each. Yeah, that's right, a food stamp. Back in the day, they came in books and there was no tax on them. All six of us would go into the store and buy something for a dime. We would all bring the change back to him. With over five dollars at a time, he could gas the car he stole from my mom via paperwork and purchase a couple joints as well. We really didn't care. We were just happy to have a pack of Lemonheads and some bubblegum to chew on.

The second thing Greg was passionate was basketball. I can't deny he was a really good basketball player. He was the best I had ever seen in my town. He introduced me to the game that eventually led me around the world and to where I am today. Early on, I didn't really care for the game, as I didn't have a lot of respect for him as a human. The game took a while to grow on me, as I found interest in other sports like baseball and football. I liked football a lot because I was small and fast. In the backyard battles, I was never easy to tackle. I loved baseball because of my Uncle Jim. Uncle Jim loved baseball more than anything in the world. He kept my grandma's TV on baseball twenty-four/seven. He was very active in our local African-American community in trying to provide baseball and other extracurricular activity for us young black kids in the projects and around town. He literally lived and died baseball. For me, baseball led me to many questions and curiosities.

The thing is, we didn't even have a real baseball field to play or practice on. We played on a field behind the old all-African-American Marian Anderson High School in my town. This was the school that all the blacks attended and graduated from until Brinkley High became integrated in the early to mid-1970s. The only thing we had was basically four dirt bases and a pitching mound. I was confused because we had such poor facilities, if we could even call them facilities. I knew we had better facilities in town because I had seen them. We all knew there were better facilities. There happened to be a problem nonetheless. The problem was that us young black kids were not allowed to play with the white kids at the local Greenlee Park. Mind you, this was the early to mid-1980s when this was happening. Why couldn't we play on the baseball teams with our white friends who we attended school with? Why couldn't we go swim at the local swimming pool with our white friends? Why were we not allowed to go skating on the weekends with our schoolmates? We had to travel twenty-five miles away to the town I was born in, Forrest City, just to skate. Why was my town so far behind in this movement? I knew it wasn't fair, and I knew it wasn't right because I had seen otherwise.

I had seen otherwise on my many summer trips to visit my dad in Dallas, Texas, over parts of my summer vacations. During those trips to South Dallas, I was able to be active with kids of all races in extracurricular activities. I was able to learn to swim! I was able to witness black kids playing on baseball teams with kids of all nationalities. During those summers, I began to realize that things in my hometown were no longer the norm. I never questioned these things, but I knew they were not normal.

I remember in elementary school feeling a sense of jealousy when my white friends would come to school wearing their baseball jerseys on days they had games. I remember reading the local newspapers praising many of the kids I went to school with on game-to-game and season accomplishments. It just wasn't fair! Who was to blame for this? Who? I certainly couldn't blame my white friends.

About five years ago, there was a feed on my Facebook from people of my hometown community. The feed read, "If you are from Brinkley, you remember when?"

Being one of the most popular people from my hometown, I decided to hit some nerves and chime in on the feed. I responded to the feed with the comment, "Then you remember when you couldn't play baseball, swim, nor could you go roller skating with your schoolmates!" As a result of me saying this I had an outpouring of inbox messages from some of the white classmates and friends I grew up with. Many of them felt the need to apologize. Many of them told me how they had no idea they lived this, but looking back, they did recall those empty voids of us black kids at many of those extracurricular activities. I gladly accepted their apologies, as I felt many of them really didn't know. They were just living victims of the ignorance that had been passed down from previous generations. Personally, I have no ill feelings toward anyone or any of the people from my town that partook in the separation that haunted our community. I'm honestly just happy things aren't like that today. I'm happy for those who realize certain things passed from our ancestors are not necessarily the way things should be.

When it comes to many things, I think it's important to think outside of the box. It's important to do research and form your own opinions. I always asked questions. I was always a little curious. This has been the basis of how I became who I am today. This is a taste of "From When I Can Remember."

CHAPTER TWO

My Sports Salvation

There are a couple of definitions of the term "salvation." The one that defines the title of this chapter for me and my sports salvation would be this one: preservation or deliverance from harm, ruin, or loss. Lifeline and/or preservation. Around the age of nine to ten, I began to see sports in this light. I began to see the possibilities of using sports to take me away from my normal everyday environment. I began to see the opportunity to possibly use the sports avenue as a lifeline.

There were several sporting events that I began to follow and pay attention to between the start of 1986 through the end of the year. Events that showed me the joy and happiness you could attain from playing sports games. The fame and the potential to be on television from playing a simple game.

I can without a doubt say the first professional team I fell in love with was the 1986 Super Bowl Champ Chicago Bears. I think the reason I fell in love with them was because of their flash and confidence. It was the first time I had ever really paid attention to an actual real professional sporting event and the days leading up to it. Seeing the highlights of Walter Payton as running back and the way he ran the football lit a fire in me. Seeing the video of the players dancing to the tune of "Super

Bowl Shuffle." I wanted to be Walter Payton of the Chicago Bears. He played the position I usually played when we played football in the backyard. I was fast, and I was small, so he was someone I could potentially grow up to be. I can remember watching that Super Bowl as the Bears easily defeated the New England Patriots. I remember how excited I was for the Bears. It was as if I had grown up and lived in Chicago! The thing was that I never lived in Chicago, but the housing projects I grew up in were located on Chicago Street. Therefore, they were my home team, for sure.

I began to become more interested in sports from this day forward. I began to pay more attention to details and the importance of learning the rules of games.

The next big sporting event that captured me was my local high school basketball team. In 1986, we had the number-one ranked basketball team in the entire state of Arkansas. This team was filled with guys who became my heroes and heroes to many kids of my town. The '86 Brinkley Tigers had gone the entire season without a loss. I can remember attending a few games at the high school gym during this amazing season and seeing news cameras on the sidelines from Little Rock just to get a few highlights of the number-one team in the state. It was awesome, to say the least. I can remember thinking that one day it could possibly be me on TV leading the Brinkley Tigers to championships.

The 1986 Tigers made it all the way to the state title game without a loss on the season. They were 26-0! There was no way I was going to miss the championship game. I didn't know how I was going to get to the game, which was an hour away in

Searcy, Arkansas, but nevertheless, I was determined to get there, as my 1986 new love for sports was at an all-time high.

Believe it or not, I made it to the game! I remember walking into the arena at Harding University in awe. It was the largest arena I had ever set foot in. Much larger than our gym in Brinkley. It was full of people! My Tigers were 26-0, and I had no doubt that like the Super Bowl Champ Chicago Bears had done a month earlier, we would be celebrating a state title. This would not be the case. I can remember the game was never close. The Hope Bobcats from southern Arkansas dominated from beginning to end.

For me, it piqued another emotion sports could trigger in me. For the first time, sports made me cry. I remember walking on the court after the game, seeing the Hope Bobcats celebrating and seeing my Tigers and all of our fans with tears in their eyes. How could this happen? We were the number-one team in the state for the entire season. We were supposed to win! I cried like a baby.

I learned a huge lesson on this night. I learned that nothing is given, and anything can happen on any given night. Nothing is given, and everything worth having must be earned. As happy as I was when the Chicago Bears won, I was equally sad and disappointed when my Brinkley Tigers took the unexpected loss.

There was light from the loss when it was all said and done. Several of the guys from this great Tiger team had earned basketball scholarships. I remember seeing in the local newspaper several of the guys from the almost undefeated Tigers were headed to college for free. I knew what a scholarship was because a few years earlier, my Aunt Nena who had gone to college on a basketball scholarship. This immediately became a goal of mine.

So much happened to me mentally this particular year. This year changed my life! I couldn't get enough of watching sports. I begin to play more sports. I was anywhere a game was to be played. Basketball, football, and baseball were my favorites. My Uncle Jim no longer had to force me to play baseball or watch it on TV. I was all in! My only wish was that we had better facilities and better organization like teams and youth organizations I would see while visiting Dallas during the summers with my dad. My town just didn't provide the funding for us, but we had several sports-enthusiastic parents in our town who did what they could to give us something to do recreationally, including my Uncle Jim. I knew I wanted trophies. I knew I wanted to compete. I wanted to be in the newspaper being praised for my accomplishments. I wanted trophies like my cousins up the road in Memphis had on their shelves from participating and winning in youth sports.

I begin to see sports and the possibilities that could result from hard work. I was beginning to notice it everywhere I went. My Grandma Mamie and I would often take the Greyhound bus an hour up to road to visit my aunt, uncle, and cousins in Memphis, Tennessee. Grandma Mamie was my dad's mom. We took many trips to Memphis on the old Greyhound bus. I loved it! For me, it was always a timely escape from the norm or my at times unpredictable childhood. Trips to Memphis allowed me to see even more possibilities. My aunt and uncle were successful. They were married, and my cousins seemed to have all they needed and more. I never wanted to leave when I would visit.

They had a hoop in the driveway, and I could play basketball all night long. When I would visit, they would have to make me come in because I never wanted to stop playing. I never wanted to stop shooting. I never wanted to stop working on my game. Right-handed lay-up, left-handed lay-up, reverse lay-ups, and so on. I didn't need anyone to play with me. I would play against the shadows. I was young Michael Jordan in my mind. I was Magic Johnson. I was a shooter like Larry Bird of the 1986 NBA World Championship Celtics! I must admit, I hated the Celtics, and I was not thrilled at all when they defeated the Houston Rockets in the championship that year, but I couldn't deny their dominance. These are the hoop dreams I played out during these moments. I would shoot in the rain. I would play when it was cold outside. I would play in the dark. It didn't matter to me. At a very young age, I was focused and determined to make it in sports. I was going to be Michael Jordan, Walter Payton, or Darryl Strawberry of the 1986 Baseball World Champion New York Mets. I automatically had love for the Mets. I had an aunt who lived in Queens. An aunt who my Grandma Haley, who was my mom's mom, took me to visit in New York when I was about four years old. We took a two-day Greyhound trip up to Queens, New York.

There have been many events since 1986 that grew my passion for sports more, but at the end of the day, the year of 1986 was truly my sports salvation. I would tell any person: It doesn't matter if you are an adult or a kid. You have to find your salvation. It's important to find things that motivate you and encourage you to get going each and every day. At a very young age, I found these things. I was able to find solace and motivation in them. I was able to set goals on these experiences, even as an adolescent. The experiences I had in this year of 1986 taught me the thrill of victory and the agony of defeat. I certainly didn't like the feeling of defeat. The feeling of defeat motivated me to work harder so I would be able to experience the thrill of victory on a more regular basis.

What's your salvation?

CHAPTER THREE

In the Game

I decided to call this chapter "In the Game" because it's when I officially had to chance to play organized sports. I would finally be able to participate in the sports I loved under the organization of the public school system. You see, in Brinkley, when you got into seventh grade, that was where it all began for most of my friends who had the love of sports. We had a chance to play organized football and basketball for the first time. In my hometown, when you made it to the seventh grade, you were officially in the big times! I was no longer going to school with elementary-age kids. My local high school consisted of grades seven through twelve. Once I reached this pinnacle, I knew I would be able to finally and potentially have a legitimate chance to have my name and photos printed in the local newspaper for excelling in the sports activities that I loved.

It all begin with football. Football, for me, was my favorite sport. As I mentioned before, I was small and fast. It was back then, and I can probably say that even now, it's my favorite sport to watch. Seventh grade began, and it, of course, began with the start of football season. I was very excited, to say the least. For me, it would be the first time I would have the chance to play tackle football with full equipment. To be honest, I don't really remember how the tryouts went for seventh-grade football. I do know that anyone who wanted to play was guaranteed a spot on the team, as we didn't have a crazy number of kids in my class to have a real tryout, per se. One thing I did know is that I was playing running back. Coach gave me the job of playing right half-back in the good ole wishbone formation, a football formation made really popular in the 1980s. It was a formation made famous by college football teams such as University of Oklahoma, Texas, and my home state favorite college football team, Arkansas Razorbacks.

My first football game experience was one to remember. It didn't go exactly as I had planned or imagined. We had our first game against the Elaine Panthers. The Panthers were another small-town Arkansas school with a population around the same as my hometown of Brinkley. We all gathered on the bus to take the one-hour trip down to Elaine on a Thursday evening. There was a bus of seventh-graders as well as the junior high football team consisting of eighth- and ninth-graders. My seventh-grade teammates and friends would be playing the first game of the night.

I remember getting ready for the game like it was yesterday. I remember strapping on the Brinkley Tiger uniform for the first time. I wore number 20. I wore the neck brace and goggles as if I were Eric Dickerson of the LA Rams. I remember the smell of the grass. I remember the pregame warmup. I even remember looking up to the scoreboard and realizing that this time the game was going to be for real! My teammates and I were all very pumped up!

In seventh-grade football, there were no kick-offs, nor were there any punts. We would get the ball first on our own thirty-five-yard line after winning the pregame coin toss. As soon as we huddled, I looked over to the opposing team and felt so nervous I thought I would vomit. That would have been super embarrassing if I had done that! Coach stepped into the huddle and called "L, sweep left." L would tell the tight end where to line up on the left side of the field, and the play would be run to that same side. It was my play! Coach called my play first on the very first game of my football career.

We lined up, and our QB got the snap from center. He tossed it over to me as I got behind my running backs, hoping to score my first touchdown. As I ran the football for the first time, I quickly realized I was running out of field on the left side, so I decided to change directions. I abandoned my block and turned sweep left into sweep right. From what I could see, there was plenty of room to roam on that side of the field. I began to pick up speed as I angled to the right side of the foot-ball field, and before I knew it, there was no one in front of me except the end zone!

I had done it! I had scored a sixty-five-yard touchdown on my very first play of my very first organized football game! No one had even touched me while running the football. I put the ball down and immediately began to celebrate. I was jumping up and down, pointing into the stands at our junior high football team as part of my end zone celebration. They were doing the same thing back at me. This was a dream come true! Well, it was a dream come true until I turned back around to the playing field. I turned back to the field to see that my best friend, Marlon, was lying on the football that I had prematurely put down on the two-yard line!

It turned out that I had not scored a touchdown. I had fumbled on the two-yard line! I couldn't believe it. Instead of a scoring a sixty-five-yard touchdown, I had run sixty-three yards and fumbled. I quickly realized that the junior high football players weren't actually celebrating with me when they were pointing. They were laughing, yelling, and pointing at me to inform me that I had fumbled! I was so embarrassed when it was all said and done. It's pretty funny looking back at almost thirty years later, but in retrospect, I would have preferred to have just thrown up in the huddle when Coach called the play for me instead of the infamous fumble. Coach ended up calling the next play on the two-yard line for the fullback. He scored my touchdown. I don't remember much of the game past our fullback scoring that touchdown. I know that we won and I had fun.

I didn't score a touchdown the entire season. I scored several two-point conversions, but no touchdowns. It seems I had cursed myself for the season. There was a silver lining in the season nonetheless. The coach of our senior high football team realized my passion for the sport and offered me a position with the big boys as one of the student managers for the team.

As a manager of the senior team, I would have many responsibilities, none of which I minded one bit! I just wanted to be a part of the game. As a manager, I would be responsible for things like preparing water for practice and games and gathering dirty laundry when the days were done. One of my favorite duties was being able to set up the football field before games. I really felt a part of something special. I felt like I was growing up. This experience as manager taught me so much.

On a daily basis, I was able to see what it took in practice preparations and coaches' meetings from week to week. I was able to sit in on film sessions. During the games, I would be on the field in the huddle with the team between timeouts, as I had to run the water for the players onto the field. It was so much fun! At a very young age, I realized that if you wanted to be good at a game, you had to do more than just play. You had to prepare and work hard! This was by far my best football year. It was a special year. As manager, I was able to be a part of an underdog Brinkley Tiger football team traveling up to Lonoke, Arkansas, to win the conference championship on the Lonoke Jackrabbits' home football field. The senior team would be headed to the state playoffs for the first time in several years, and I was there to experience and celebrate it. That football season would end in a first-round defeat, but it was memorable, to say the least. It wasn't sad when the season was over because I had something else to look forward to. I had basketball just around the corner!

Basketball tryouts were much like football tryouts in the seventh grade. There weren't really any tryouts! Coach Williams, who was my basketball coach, pretty much gave a uniform to anyone who wanted to play. Coach Williams was the coach of all things boys basketball at Brinkley High. He was the coach that led our 1986 Brinkley Tiger basketball team to the magical 26-1 state runner-up season. It was immediately a pleasure and an honor to have him as my basketball coach. From day one, Coach Williams was a motivator and mentor to me. It didn't hurt that his son Marlon was in the same grade as me and my best friend.

In seventh-grade basketball, I would take on the same role as I had taken during football season. I would play basketball for the seventh-grade basketball team, and I would also be allowed to be a manager and travel with the senior high basketball team. Coach Williams gave me my first nickname. He called me "Lang Bang." Whenever I would shoot the basketball, he would call my name, Lang, and if the shot went in, he would end it with "Bang." Athletes and peers around school started calling me by that name. It was pretty cool to have a nickname. I had officially arrived. I was a seventh-grader with a cool nickname.

Seventh-grade basketball was really fun. I was what you would call a scrapper. I was small, but I would get all the steals, long rebounds, and loose balls during the course of the game. I was really good at anticipating. I learned this playing in the park with the big guys at a young age. I knew when I played with the big boys in the park that I couldn't rebound under the hoop, so I learned how to read how the ball would come off the rim, and I could always quickly get to the basketball. I was fast and I was small in seventh grade, standing a whopping five foot two inches.

My first season of basketball was pretty similar to my first organized football experience, except I didn't have any embarrassing moments similar to the premature football celebration. We would travel to some games with the junior high basketball team and play before them as we had during football. It was a process of making lots of new and first memories as well as developing friendships that would last a lifetime.

Being at the high school playing sports and being in the game was exactly what I needed. I didn't really focus anymore on any issues I had to deal with away from school and sports. Sports were the perfect distraction for me. Once I had arrived, I no longer had to deal with being picked on as much for things such as my appearance or material things that I just didn't have. I began to find myself this seventh-grade year. People back then and still today treat you differently when you are good at something. I was pretty good at a couple of things, and I knew it at this point in my life. For all of the awesome things I had experienced in this year, it seemed that the year had flown by! It was summer before I knew it.

Every kid enjoyed summer. In the past, summer for me meant traveling to Dallas to spend time with my dad. This summer would be different. This summer, I was adamant about spending the summer in Brinkley with my friends. The other thing about this summer was that it would be the first opportunity for me to attend basketball camp in Searcy, Arkansas—the same place I had watched our 1986 basketball team lose in the state championship. Searcy was a college town and home of the Harding University Bison. This summer trip would become an annual thing for my basketball teammates and me all the way through our high school days. Basketball camp was my first real summer vacation experience, so to speak. Coach Williams encouraged all of his upcoming eighth- and ninth-graders to attend this particular basketball camp.

The only problem I initially had with the camp was trying to figure out how I could convince my mom to come off $125 to pay for the week of improving my basketball skills. It wasn't as hard as I thought it would be. For the many disagreements and run-ins we'd had to this point in my life, she always figured out a way to make sure I got all the things I wanted and needed.

For me, basketball camp at Harding was my first taste of what it was like to be a college student, as we would be sleeping in the dorms and eating at the university cafeteria just the same as the college kids who were in summer school. Harding was also the University that two of the best players from the 1986 Tigers basketball were attending. They actually worked the camps. I was able to attend basketball camp at the university that outfitted a couple of my hometown heroes. While attending basketball camp, I was able to hang out with and pick the brains of actual college basketball players. I remember a few of them telling me stories about when they started playing sports and all the important steps they took to get to where they were, including the importance of making good grades. I didn't really make bad grades at this point of my life, but I knew from what they were telling me that I eventually had to do better. Basketball camp was certainly a success in the knowledge I was able to gather. I learned many basic fundamentals of the game that I had no idea about, things I would be able to go home and work on in my downtime. I learned so much in such a short period time. I learned things that would not only help me in basketball but would help me in life and in sports in general.

Summer passed, and the new school year began. I was now an eighth-grader playing on the junior teams with the ninth-graders. This was for basketball and football. As an eighth-grader, it was hard to get playing time over a ninth-grader in any sport. In football as an eighth-grader, I was the back-up fullback. I thought I was better than the guy in front of me, but I never made a fuss, as I knew my time would come, and I knew the importance of being a good teammate.

Basketball was different because Coach Williams was known for running a platoon-type of substitution pattern. Playing time was not an issue. Coach Williams had begun to pattern his coaching style to one similar to the Arkansas Razorbacks' coach at that time, Nolan Richardson. Nolan ran what he called forty minutes of hell, and that was what my coach wanted as well, except it was more like twenty-four minutes of hell since we only played six minutes per quarter. It didn't matter because Coach would start the ninth-graders and about halfway through each quarter, he would substitute the next five eighth-graders into the games; I was in that eighth-grade crew. We were expected to go in and pick up where the upper classmen had left off, and that's exactly what we did. We would pick up full court and press the opposition team for as long as we were in the game. There was not much of a drop off from us eighth-graders and the ninth-graders. They were better than us, but not by much.

This would be the first season that I would be a part of a championship team as a player. This year, we would finish the basketball season at 14-2 and as champions of the conference. Coach called us the "beast of the east," as Brinkley sits in eastern Arkansas. For as much as he praised us, he also made sure we knew to never be satisfied. As eighth-graders, we immediately set the goal of going undefeated as freshmen, but first we had to get ready for the summer and our second trip to Harding Summer Basketball Camp. This would be a summer camp I would never forget.

I was now a summer camp veteran. By the time summer camp rolled around, I had grown to a measly five foot four, but still, I was fast and I could shoot, making up for what I lacked in height. Speed and my shooting ability would be all I needed to accomplish the goal I had set going into basketball camp that summer. One thing I didn't mention about the first time I attended was awards day. There were several awards handed out on the final day of basketball camp. They were handed to the players who had displayed certain skills during the actual games as well as individual contest set up by camp staff. I was determined to win something, and boy, did I accomplish this goal.

It started with a dribbling contest. This was nothing more than an obstacle course with the winner being the player that could maneuver around the course with the fastest time. When all the campers had gone, it was me who had the fastest time. Next, we had the free throw shooting contest, which I was also able to win. I had already exceeded my goal of winning an award. I had won two awards with two more contests ahead of me. After the free throw shooting contest was shooting three pointers. I was in the zone! I couldn't miss! With winning the three-point contest, I had won three events in a row. Finally, the contest left was one on one. I just knew there was no way I was going to win this. I was too small, and guys could easily back me down and shoot lay-ups. Somehow, I had shot and maneuvered my way down to the championship game, and I would face my best friend, Marlon, who had about eight inches on me; he stood about six feet tall going into the ninth grade. Marlon was a really good player. We played many one-on-one games even before basketball camp. He would win some games, and I would win some. This was just to be my day! It was a close game that came down to the last shot, which I eventually made.

I had made a clean sweep of the awards at summer basketball camp. I couldn't have imagined this happening, but it did. I left basketball camp with six t-shirts. I was dribble, free-throw, three-point, one-on-one, and not to mention the hustle award winner! The camp staff gave me the hustle award, as they said they had never seen a kid hustle and play as hard as I did. I was so excited to get back home and tell my mom the news. I felt bad that my best friend didn't get any of the awards, but it was just my day. When we got home from camp, our local newspaper came out to take a photo of all of us who had attended camp. I remember reading in the paper all of the names and seeing our photo, but also the newspaper mentioning how I had made a clean sweep of all of the camp awards. I had reached a goal. I had finally made the newspaper, and it was a result of my determination and hard work. I have to admit, I kind of got a big head!

There is not much I remember from my freshman year of high school except being humbled. I had a pretty good freshman year playing football, but basketball was another story. I begin the season as a starter but eventually went to a stretch of about six or seven games that Coach Williams didn't even play a couple of my teammates and good friends. He felt we weren't working hard and didn't want us to develop the mentality that things should be handed to us just because. I didn't understand why he was doing this when it was happening, but looking back, I know he was absolutely correct!

I had learned so much over these past couple of years. I learned what it would take to reach some of my ultimate goals. I learned what it took to get in the game. More so than getting in the game, I learned what it took to stay in the game. Coach Williams taught me this the hard way, but in a way that would pay off.

My freshmen year, I remember Coach telling all of us that freshman year through senior year would be the most important years of our young lives. The grades that we made starting freshman year would be the ones to follow us for the rest of our lives, and they would determine whether or not we would be able to get into college after high school. This was the one thing I did take to heart. As I stated earlier, I had not made bad grades, but I needed to do better. Basketball season as a freshman didn't go exactly as I had planned, but I made the newspaper for other reasons. I made the newspaper for being on honor roll! I was more than in the game!

CHAPTER FOUR

Making the Grade

Sally Loretz was one of my first history teachers. She was one of the first of many teachers when I was entering high school who showed faith in me. She made a deal with me. The governor of Arkansas was coming to visit our school. To be honest, I didn't really care or even knew who the governor was at this time. She proposed to me that if I could remember all of the names of the presidents of the United States, when the governor visited our school, she would make sure I had a seat on the aisle. I didn't care much about this proposal, but it was a challenge and deal I accepted. I met her challenge! For a test, I was able to get all of the names of the presidents correct and in order. I got a perfect score! I didn't really think much of it, but when the governor visited, I was to be seated in the aisle.

You may ask, why was this important to me? I honestly can't remember or say why, but it was a challenge. Mrs. Loretz was a happy and fun teacher I enjoyed who found fun little ways of challenging and motivating me. Governor Bill Clinton was the man who would be coming to my school to speak. I remember being amazed and captivated by the buzz that the governor was at my school. He was at Brinkley High, and I had an aisle seat as he made his way into our auditorium with a crazy amount of security. I didn't realize the importance of the governor until that moment.

The governor no doubt gave an amazing, motivational speech to all of us in attendance that day. He talked about the importance of many things. He stressed the importance of being confident, proud, humble, and the importance of never giving up on dreams. Like me, the governor was from a small town. He was from the town of Hope in southern Arkansas. The same town that had defeated my 1986 undefeated Brinkley Tigers basketball team. This really didn't matter to me, though. What mattered to me after he left was that I'd sat on the aisle. When he finished his speech and made his way out of our auditorium, he walked down the middle aisle where I was sitting, and I was able to shake his hand. The governor shook my hand! It was the first important person I had ever met at this point in my life. I had no idea that he would one day in the near future become president of the United States, but of course he did. He shook my hand! I met and shook hands with a man who was the governor and future president of the United States!

I had no idea what the future held for him, nor did I know what the future held for me, but like my basketball coach stressed entering high school, education was the key! Coach Williams always stressed education first. I was best friends with his son, Marlon, and he always motivated me to work hard regardless of how small I was. Coach knew both of my parents because he had taught both of them during their time in school. He knew they were pretty tall. Taller than the average man and woman. He used to tell Marlon and me that one day, I would be taller than Marlon because both of my par-

28

ents were taller than average. My mom was five foot ten, and my dad was six foot one. I just didn't believe it! More importantly, he stressed making the grade. He had coached so much talent over the years that had never gotten out of our small town because of the simple fact that they just were not focused on making the grade. For many, it was never about their talent in sports. It was more about them being coachable and teachable. This was pounded into my brain from him on the regular.

When I was a sophomore in high school, I was still small compared to most of the guys I played basketball with. I decided I wouldn't play football that year. I'm not exactly sure why I chose not to play, but I didn't. I had expected in that year I would be able to contribute to the basketball team more than the football team. It ended up not being the year I expected with basketball, but I was still determined and focused. Over the summer, I had regretted my decision not to play football this particular year because, in hindsight, I didn't get any playing time on the basketball court. My basketball court time was about the same as my football time! It was almost zero, and I didn't even play football. Nonetheless, I still went to basketball camp in the summer following my sophomore year of high school. It was just the thing to do, and I really loved the game of basketball. I loved basketball and football equally at this point in my life. Besides, I wasn't growing any, so over the summer, I had in my mind even after attending basketball team camp that I missed playing the game of football. I had to make a decision this summer that had to be mine. I had to decide if I would continue to only focus on basketball or if I would go back to my first sport—my love of football.

The decision was made about two weeks before the start of the school year. I had decided for my junior year that I would rejoin the football team. It wasn't really a tough decision considering I felt I had wasted a year by not playing football and not contributing to the basketball team. I was totally good regardless because I had made the honor roll my entire sophomore year! My grades were good enough to where I was even able to replace my study hall class with a job of working across the block as a tutor for the elementary school. Education was literally paying off for me in more ways than one. I was able to play football as a junior and help kids down the school block as a tutor for one of my favorite teachers who had also taught me back in the day.

I still hadn't grown much in stature, but I was a good and smart athlete. My junior year of high school, I still stood five foot seven or five foot eight on a good day, but I was still no doubt athletic and one of the hardest workers you would find at the age of sixteen. My experience as a manager for many years for the football team would pay off this football season. I had learned so much from my years as the football team manager. I knew how to do everything, and I had a great memory. I could do anything on the football field. I could punt the football if Coach needed that. I could play quarterback as a backup if Coach needed. I could deep snap to the punter if it wasn't me punting. I could kick extra points and field goals. There was so much I could do! This was all a plus for me, especially since we only had about twenty players who came out for football on this particular season. We had guys that should have been wide receivers on our offensive and defensive lines, but lack of numbers forced many players to play out of position. We had to just get people on the field!

It was a fun year! We didn't win many games, but none of us could ever complain about playing time. We all basically played the entire game. For me, this could not all have happened without sacrifice. I had to sacrifice my ankles! As a junior on the high school football team, I had many positions. I played defensive back, wide receiver, deep snapper for the punts, and field goal kicker. I literally never left the football field, and I loved it! I was also subsequently having growing pains that I didn't know about at the time. I couldn't understand why I was always in such pain around my ankles. My football coaches couldn't really explain the problems either. It was just thought that I had bad ankles. I had begun to believe that I really had bad ankles. To be honest, it didn't really matter to me because I knew I loved football and would play no matter what, regardless of any pain endured while playing.

I had a good year playing the game I'd missed the year before. We finished with the same amount of losses as wins that year, but it was fun, and I realized I had probably made a mistake not playing the previous season as a tenth-grader. I had actually gotten playing time as a football player, unlike the time I had received as a tenth-grade basketball player.

Of course, there was a problem with this football season. For all I had done for the team that season, I was feeling a bit unappreciated. When the season-ending football banquet came around, I left really disappointed. I remember being super heartbroken when I left the banquet. I was in tears. For all I had done for the football team, the only thing I was awarded was a letterman jacket. There were guys who had received many awards and trophies. I had no trophies! No one knew, but immediately when the ceremony was over and everyone was dismissed, I walked away and to my grandparents' house in tears, even leaving the letterman jacket at the ceremony. I didn't even want it. This left a sour taste in my mouth. How could I do so much and not be recognized?

This left me really motivated for basketball and the start of the season. At this point, I was still mini at five foot eight, but now I had a real chip on my shoulder to prove that I was worthy and needed to be recognized for my abilities and contributions. Why was I having to deal with this? It was because I needed to grow! I needed to grow mentally and physically.

Once basketball started, I no longer had ankle issues. I was a pretty damn good basketball player as a junior! The rotation that Coach Williams had working worked for me. Five players in and five players out allotted me lots of playing time. We had a really good basketball team that year. We didn't meet our goals, but like every year I was in high school, we won our conference and advanced to the state playoffs. Although we didn't happen to win state, I did one thing I had never done in a basketball game. I dunked. It was like a dream!

It happened on a play we called snow birding. We were playing against the team I had played my very first organized basketball game against, the Marvell Mustangs. With the game in control, Coach decided to put a couple juniors in the game, including me. He told me to just wait around half-court for the ball if the opposition missed, and me being so damn coachable, I did exactly as he asked. They shot and missed. My teammate Tyrone Butler got the rebound and basketball passed it to me just past half-court. There was no one between me and the basket. I remember catching the ball and taking maybe two dribbles. It happened! I slam dunked! I was giving high-fives to all of our fans who were hanging over the rails of our gym. That's all I remember from that night. I had dunked at five foot eight!

The next day at school was crazy. The students who had attended the game the previous night showed me so much love. This love didn't stop at the high school. The kids who I tutored daily who were at the game that night went crazy when I came to work during my study hall tutor period. I realized at this point that I had a chance to be different. I could make the grade and do things that were not so normal around where I came from. I was able to be respected in my high school, and at the same time, kids in my elementary school looked up to me.

I had made the grade! I had made the grades in my books, and I made the grades on the basketball court. I was now at least one step closer to realizing my dream of going to college. Going to college was at least a year away, but grades and sports made it appear to be something I would potentially be able to accomplish as a result of one or the other. Little ole me had met a future USA president, overcome ankle issues, and slam dunked while making the grade! What next? Hmm . . . Anything, because I had realized the sky could be the limit for me!

CHAPTER FIVE

Decisions, Decisions, Decisions

Going into the end of my junior year of high school and transitioning into my senior year, I would be faced with many decisions that would be major in my life going forward and the journey that was ahead of me. My season of basketball as a junior had ended, and I was beginning to notice I was growing. I was having some minor growing pains, but I began to notice I was catching up and passing some of my best friends in height as the year came to an end. This would work out well for me, especially with summer basketball camp being something I was looking forward to.

My best friend, Marlon, and I would spend hours in the gym after school shooting and trying to dunk in preparation for camp. The difference at this point is that I was no longer just the guy who stood under the basket and tossed the ball to the rim for Marlon to dunk. He was now tossing the ball to me. He was tossing it to me the same way I had been tossing him ally oops as far back as seventh grade! I had caught up with him in height. It was something Coach Williams had forecasted many years back, much to my disbelief. Finally, my height had caught up with my athletic ability as we were preparing for our annual summer team basketball camp at Harding University.

As a basketball player, I was always a point guard. I was the guy who could defend the ball, shoot, and find the open man with the basketball. I was what they also called a "ball hawk." This meant I was always around the ball. No one could match my determination on defense and the effort of getting loose balls. I was really good at stealing the ball from opposition players, which led to many layups. During summer basketball camp this year, these layups would turn into slam-dunks. I imagine we played about ten games at basketball camp that summer, and I was averaging at least two dunks per game along with about twenty points every time we laced up our shoes. I had a pretty good idea after this summer that I would at least be able to get a scholarship somewhere playing basketball. Summer basketball camp, along with some of the exposure I had received playing AAU basketball for my Arkansas Lakers team, gave me the experience and the level of competition I needed to realize I was a decent basketball player.

I have to give all the credit in the world to Coach Williams for always driving Marlon and me to all of the AAU games and practices in Little Rock. Without him, there would have been no way I could have had that experience with AAU basketball. While giving Coach the credit for these efforts, I also have to give him credit for convincing me to make one of the toughest decisions I ever had to make. He didn't want me to play football as a senior. This was a hard pill for me to swallow, especially with football being my first love. I had played football before any other sport! Marlon, who, again, was Coach's son, hadn't been allowed to play football since after ninth grade. Marlon was probably one of the best wide receivers I had seen during my junior-high football days, but Coach decided Marlon had enough of football and it was time for him to focus on basketball after freshman year.

Oftentimes, Coach looked at me and treated me like a son. He just never had the leverage to decide what I could and couldn't do. I'm sure if he had, he would have kept me off the football field after freshman year as well. Going into senior year, I had my mind made up that I was going to play football as a high school senior. Coach had a different plan for me. He told me that if I played football, I wouldn't be getting any playing time during basketball season. This all had me shook! Why did he not want me to play football? Was it because of the ankle problems I had the previous year, or did he just think he could scare me out of playing? We had several guys that played both sports, and he couldn't care less that they played both sports. He actually encouraged them to play football. A couple of the guys were key starters on our projected senior basketball starting lineup. It didn't matter to Coach. His idea was those guys could play football and basketball and I couldn't. We had a bit of an argument about it. I said my peace, and Coach said his.

When the summer came to an end and football physicals and practice came around, I was one of the first down to the field house to get my football physical. I was playing football whether Coach liked it or not! A few days after the physicals had been administered, football practice time came around. I never made it to football practice! The decision had been made. I wasn't going to play football. I'm not sure exactly what triggered me not to go to that first day of football practice, but it didn't happen. Maybe it was the idea of the pain I felt in my ankles the previous season along with the one-hundred-degree temperatures during two-a-day practices.

Needless to say, Coach Williams was pleased with my decision. As a bit of a reward for me not playing football, Coach would take me with him and Marlon to every road football game during the football season my senior year. Marlon had an old Mazda RX-7 that was a two-seater hatchback. You might be wondering why the style of this car is relevant. Well, it's because for these road games, I would fold my six-foot-two-inch body in the hatch of this small car and ride for hours at a time just to be at the football games. I have no idea how I managed. I guess it was simply for the love of the game, but I did it. In hindsight, it was pretty crazy, but I have some great memories from back there in the RX-7 nonetheless.

The start of my senior year was interesting, to say the least. I had been selected to be president of my senior class without even running much of a campaign. I think my classmates had just begun to recognize me as a leader in everything I took part in. During the football pep rallies, there was not a student in my class who made more noise at those weekly events than me. We had the smallest class in the school, so we would never win the pep rally, but it still didn't stop me from trying to rally my classmates into showing school spirit! It was always about effort and energy with me. I was super competitive and didn't want to lose at anything. Not even a pep rally!

Even with all the leadership and work I put into things, it didn't seem early on that I would be rewarded. I thought it would be realistic that I get a scholarship, but I wasn't seeing any signs of this happening. I had not received any pre-basketball-season scholarship offers to my knowledge. This was really frustrating, especially knowing how history had shown me many guys had boxes of letters from different schools that recruited potential student athletes.

I was still positive in my outlook on things. I was ready to get the basketball season started. I was in the best basketball shape of my life, and I had put in the work. I just needed someone or a school to come and see me in action. I needed schools to see what I was doing on the court. Coach had the idea that if you make it to state, you will be seen. This was a great theory, but what if we didn't make it? Things happen! I felt that he needed to be inviting coaches in to see us play. Coach was pretty old school in that he didn't allow our games to even be video recorded. One of my teammates' dad who we called "Snowman" would sneak and film a few games anyway. I was thrilled at this because I figured if things didn't go as planned, I would at least have some action on tape to present to some colleges and universities. Regardless of these seemingly minor issues, basketball season was off to a really good start, especially around the Christmas break games.

Two things happened to me—one good and one that, at the time, I considered pretty bad. The bad thing is that my longtime girlfriend decided to break up with me. We had been dating pretty much all of my high school days until one day around Christmas break when she decided it was all over. She had been doing a bit of parading around town with one of my buddies. This knocked me off my feet for a few seconds, but I was quick to bounce back from this. I was extra motivated. I was going to make her regret the decision she'd made. Merry

Christmas to me! (I say that with extreme sarcasm.) That was the bad thing that happened over the break, but don't forget the good. A blessing in disguise had showed up for a couple of games over Christmas break. His name was Walter Camper.

Walter was a kid I had grown up with in Brinkley. He was a couple of years older than me, also the younger brother of the best player on the 1986 undefeated Brinkley High School Basketball team, Corey Camper. Walter was a really good basketball player in his own right. After his sophomore season at Brinkley High, he had transferred to a bigger school in the capital city of Little Rock. During his two years in Little Rock, he quickly gained the reputation as a guy who could really score the basketball, thus leading him to a basketball scholarship to NCAA division-one school Centenary College, located in Shreveport, Louisiana. Walter played AAU basketball with the likes of future NBA stars Corliss Williamson and Derek Fisher. Walter was one of the first guys from my hometown to go on and play division-one basketball. He didn't graduate from Brinkley but was still a hometown hero for his accomplishments.

As a freshman at Centenary, Walter had suffered a devastating injury that caused him to miss his entire sophomore season. This was oddly a blessing in disguise for me. This gave Walter the chance to come home over the Christmas break to visit family as well as catch a couple of my games. Once I noticed him in the stands at our first home game over Christmas break, I knew it was time for me to show up and show out. I knew it was a chance for me to be seen by someone I looked up to. That first game Walter attended, I had about thirty-five points with at least three dunks during the game. I can remember him along with many of our other supporters leaning over the bleacher rails giving us high-fives during and after the game. His being there motivated me.

He came to the next game, and the result was to be no different. I played just as well as I had during the first game he attended. He said to me after the game, "I'm going to tell them about you!" To me, this meant he was going to go back to college and tell the coaches at Centenary what he had discovered while home over Christmas break. Could this be? Could this be the person I needed to discover me since at this point no school was actively recruiting me and the season was halfway over? All I knew was that my motivation was at an all-time high. I knew I had been seen!

Along with playing some good basketball, I moved on to a new girlfriend—a girl I had been friends with since childhood. We'd often flirted over the years, but the timing hadn't really coincided until after Christmas break of this particular year. She was the one I had always wanted all along. It was a blessing in disguise. I was a senior in high school with things seeming to be at an all-time high. I had the girl I wanted, and my basketball as well as my grades were on point.

Basketball season went along to be good, not great. It didn't end the way we had hoped. We won the conference that year but eventually got knocked out of the first round of the playoffs. We no doubt had one of the best teams in the state in our classification, but certain circumstances didn't allow us to complete our ultimate goal of winning the state championship.

All was not lost. It turned out there were a couple of schools that were interested in giving me and Marlon basketball scholarships. I had the grades, and I had qualified by making the required score on the ACT. I had two scholarship offers. Both of the schools were NAIA schools. One was Harding University, which was the place I had spent all of my summers attending basketball camp. The other school was the University of Arkansas at Monticello, which my Aunt Nena had played for in the early 1980s.

I was grateful and honored to have these schools show interest in me, but my real goal was to play NCAA division-one basketball. It seemed this was not going to happen until like clockwork I got the call from Centenary. It seemed that Walter had come through for me. Walter and his dad, Walter, Sr., had put a word in for me good enough to where Centenary was offering me a full basketball scholarship without ever having seen me play a game. They had never seen me play, but they knew the accolades I had accomplished over my senior year; I had been selected player of the year in my conference, had been all state, and had been selected to play in the state all-star game. This a game only the top players in the state would be allowed to participate in. When I got the call from Centenary, I only had one question: where do I sign? They told me they would like to fly me down to Shreveport for a recruiting visit before I made my final decision. This was not necessary, but I flew down anyway to see the campus. I didn't care if I liked the place or not; I knew I wanted to go there to fulfill my dream of playing NCAA division-one basketball. The recruiting visit went well, and within days of returning from the visit, I signed my letter of intent to accept the scholarship offer. It was a dream come true! I was going to play basketball at the highest level in college, and it was all because of my hard work and having someone speak up for me.

Still today, I often recall and remind people how important it is to be good toward people at all times. You never know when you will need someone. You never know who you will need. Because of the way I carried myself on the court and in the classroom, Walter and Mr. Camper stuck their name and word on the line to get me a scholarship, and for them, I am forever grateful today and forevermore! I am grateful for Coach Williams always supporting me and trying to lead me in the right direction. These are a couple of the people who helped carve the life and the future that would be in front of me. I think you would agree that my senior year had overall been a success.

When I was in seventh grade, I recall taking a class called "Career Orientation." I remember telling the teacher that I wanted to be a professional athlete. She said to me, "You have a better chance of winning the lottery!" After that comment, she guided me to the files of many possible careers and encouraged me to look through the files. In reality, she was absolutely right in her assumption, but with me gaining a full scholarship to play basketball at Centenary, I was one step closer to attaining this possibility of achieving one of my goals.

In my senior class, when all was said and done, Marlon had accepted a basketball scholarship to Arkansas-Monticello, and two of my other friends had accepted football scholarships. These were all huge accomplishments. You see, we only had sixty people in our graduating class, and for us to have four guys get full scholarships in sports was unheard of. All of these guys were my best friends! Friends whom I associated myself with for many reasons, one of which were similar goals. We knew we were good athletes, but we also knew the importance of making good grades in that we could get scholarships with or without sports. Along with getting the scholarships, we all also graduated with honors. Most distinguished high school honor graduates!

Decisions are not always easy. Decisions need to be well thought out. You also need to have a plan and try to stick with it as much as you can. In life, we are faced with many decisions. I am a true believer that once you make a decision, you should roll with it and work as hard as you can with whatever it is you have decided to do. I didn't originally agree with my coach's suggestion of me not playing football my senior year, but it eventually led me to where I needed to be, and that would a be acting as a future basketball player for the Centenary College Gents. The smallest NCAA division-one school in the nation, but indeed a division-one school!

Now it was time for me to get mentally prepared for all of the things that lay ahead for me in college life! To be straightforward and honest, I had many emotions as I begin to mentally prepare for this journey, but the decision of what I was transitioning into had been made, and I was determined to make the most of my first once-in-a-lifetime opportunity.

CHAPTER SIX

The Transition

The day I graduated high school was my one of the happiest days of my life. I had completed my first major goal in life. It was weird at first when I realized I didn't have to get up at 6:00 a.m. to get ready for school. The reality set in the first time all of my five younger siblings were up and getting ready for school and I was just up watching the morning news. You see, as a graduating senior, the school year ended a week or so earlier than the rest of the students. I felt grown!

I didn't really know what to do with myself, but my future stepfather did. Westley had an idea of what to do with me. It wasn't long before I was getting up at 6:00 a.m. all over again during the summer, except this time it was to go work on the fish farm. Westley was a self-employed business owner. Over the course of his life, he had picked up the trade of working with fiberglass and fish farming.

I had worked with him sparingly over past summers, but I can honestly say I didn't love it. It was good for me, nonetheless. Wesley was one of if not the only African-American fish farmer in the entire state of Arkansas. He also owned his own fiberglass business building fiberglass fish-transporting tanks that people from all over the USA ordered, being that they were in the fish farming business. In the fiberglass business, he also built canoes and could repair anything fiberglass.

I stayed away from the fiberglass and worked only on the fish farm. This was not easy work. It was for sure manual labor. I would just mentally focus my mind to convince myself that the work was just a physical workout. Back then, working on the fish farm took a lot of strength and power. Retrieving the fish from the ponds required extremely long nets with a floating cork line across the top and a heavy lead line on the bottom to drag the bottom of the ponds. The actual device is called a seine. We would have at least two people on each end, and we would drag acres of ponds, pulling the seine to capture the fish. I have no doubt this was a job that helped me increase my vertical jump even more over that summer. It was a job that taught me hard work, and it also taught me that I needed to get a college degree because I knew I didn't want to do manual labor all of my life. These ponds were often filled with fish, of course, but also snakes, frogs, and any other type of wild water creatures you could imagine. Regardless of how hard the work might have been, I was grateful to have a chance to rack up some cash before heading off to college. This was just one of the jobs I inherited over this summer before college.

My other job was working for my girlfriend's mom. My girlfriend's mom was the sole owner of the biggest African-American funeral home in town. I say I inherited this job because of the way it first went down. It was pretty funny. I was home relaxing one summer day, and the phone rang. My mom answered the phone, then proceeded to hand it to me, saying, "Mrs. Wallace wants to speak with you." Mrs. Wallace was my girlfriend's mom and the owner of the funeral home previously mentioned. She was an older lady, being around seventy at the time, and was known for being outspoken in saying whatever, everything, and anything that came to her mind. I answered the phone with a simple hello.

Mrs. Wallace said to me, "Seneca," "Pooh is headed to your house to pick you up so y'all can head to Holly Grove and pick up this dead body!"

I said, "Huh!"

Excuse my language here, as I am quoting her every word. She said, "Nigga who say 'huh' can hear!" She repeated, "I said, Pooh is headed to your house to pick you up so y'all can head to Holly Grove and pick up this dead body!"

I went mute. I was afraid of dead bodies! I was afraid to even walk past a cemetery, and now this lady was telling me I had to go pick up a dead body.

The silence broke as Mrs. Wallace spoke again. "If you gonna be part of this family, then you gonna have to learn the family business!" After that last comment, Mrs. Wallace hung up the phone. I couldn't get a word in. To be honest, I quickly forgot about having to pick up the dead body. I was thinking of how I was going to break up with my girlfriend when she showed up at my house in the funeral home hearse.

When she finally got to my house, we actually didn't break up. I got into the driver's side and headed off to Holly Grove to pick up the body. I will never forget that day. I will spare the details, as the lady was really old and had been bedridden for several years, said the vivid bedsores on her hips. We retrieved the body and dropped it off at the funeral home. After leaving

47

the funeral home, we drove back to my girlfriend's home in the hearse, completing my first deceased pickup.

When I walked into her house, her mom handed me a fifty-dollar bill and said, "There is more where that came from!"

I thought to myself, *This might not be so bad*. That was pretty easy work except for the mental aspect of the job, and I didn't even have to fight off any snakes as I did while working on the fish farm. That was my introduction to the funeral business and another mental transition into real life. I went from almost breaking up with my girlfriend over her mom's sudden proposal to doing everything in that business except embalming, which I couldn't do unless I had gone to school and been licensed to perform. I wasn't really interested in that aspect, but over this summer, my relationship with my girlfriend grew stronger. As much as I was looking forward to heading off to college, I was not looking forward to leaving her behind, as she still had one more year of high school to complete. We had planned to make our relationship work in the meantime as the summer came to an end and off to college I went.

The day had finally come for me to leave Brinkley and head off to college. First-year college students had to report a few days earlier prior to the actual start day of school for orientation. I loaded up the car Wesley had gotten for me, which was a 1991 Dodge Dynasty. It was a family car and not exactly the kind of car a kid takes to school, but it was clean and perfect for my needs, so I was grateful.

The directions to Shreveport were given to me by my buddy Walter. He said it would take me about four hours to get there. This was before the days of all the fancy navigation tools we have today. I was a bit nervous and excited for the drive since the only other time I had been to Shreveport was for my recruiting visit. I eventually made my way down to Shreveport, arriving with no issues. I pulled up to campus, first stopping at the athletic offices so the coaches and staff could get me situated in the dorm.

After I arrived, they quickly led me to the dorm which would be my new home. They also let me know which of my teammates would be my roommate: Lincoln Abrams. Like myself, "Link" was from Arkansas. He was a junior college transfer, meaning he had already done two years of college at a previous college. We had met on my recruiting visit, although we hadn't spoken much. Link was older than I was. I had just turned eighteen, and he was already twenty-one, entering his junior year of college at Centenary.

The first day got off to a shaky start as he tried to establish himself as the alpha male of the room. We nipped that in the bud quickly, and we would never have any issues from that first day forward. The first day was really eye-opening for me.

I already knew that my school was predominately white, but it was even more so than I imagined. It was totally different from what I was used to back home in Brinkley. I was used to seeing kids have nice cars and clothes back home but not to the level of some of these college kids. Several of them were driving cars the likes of Mercedes, BMWs, and souped-up trucks. Seeing this for the first time triggered my mind back to one of the many talks good ole Coach Williams had given me. He often talked about the importance of being hungry and working for things. He said if you already had everything given to you, then you wouldn't be as motivated to work for things. I knew that these kids had not worked for these super nice things. I knew they probably came from families with money who could provide these luxuries. Most of the kids at Centenary were super smart and motivated regardless of the material things they possessed, but for me, I knew I wanted to be able to have access so some of these fine life luxuries somewhere down the line in life.

Coach talked to me about the importance of being focused once I arrived to campus. He forewarned me about how things would be when I stepped on campus and the importance of being consistent and aware during the initial weeks and months. When it came down to things like partying and drinking, Coach would say that if you did all of those things while you were young, what would you have to look forward to when you got older? This was another thing I did see early on. When I got to Louisiana, the legal drinking age was eighteen, and there were plenty of kids drinking at this age, including many of my fellow college athletes on campus. This was an activity I for certain didn't take part in. Coach talked about how many kids would get to college and party it up, and before they knew it, they were back home because they had failed out of school. I knew I didn't want this to be me, so I made sure I stayed away from the partying. I didn't even attend the parties that would happen in the dorms.

The first weekend was pretty wild, from my recollections. Upperclassmen had finally arrived, and I imagine it was because it was a new year and everyone was really happy to see one another after the summer break.

All I knew was that I missed my girlfriend back home and I would be heading home the next weekend and every weekend after if I didn't have any practices, which I didn't. The

NCAA had a particular date for us basketball student-athletes to begin organized practices, so the weekends were free up until October 15. I went home every weekend up until that weekend. I heard I broke the record for the most consecutive weekend trips home. The previous record, according to my new teammates, was four weekends in a row. I smashed that record with eight consecutive weekend trips home, mainly to see my girlfriend.

College was going great for the most part. I wasn't homesick at all. I guess early on I had not been away from home long enough to get homesick. College life was great. I didn't have to be sitting in classrooms seven hours per day as I did in high school. I had my classes scheduled so I could get a daily power nap in. It was all good. The main thing was the assignments. In college, I wasn't spending as much time in classes per se, but the reading projects and reading assignments outside of classwork were pretty demanding. I actually had to read books! I had never really read any books during high school. That was not something we did in high school.

In college, the dynamic of the class was much different from what I was used too. At Centenary, I would often be the only black kid in class. This was really tough at first, as I was pretty shy and laid-back. I was in a shell. Early on, I didn't really take part in many of the class open discussions, as I found it hard to relate to many of the students and the things being discussed. This was a process that was gradual for me. Eventually, as I got more comfortable, I began to open up more, expanding my mental diversity. It was an entirely different type of diversity than I was used to. Centenary wasn't diverse as in being equally divided into many different races, but diverse in a way that was new and good to me. Early on, I had become friends with whites, Asians, and Latino students, just name a few cultures new to me. People from walks of life with which I had never interacted. This was one of the greatest things I took from college.

I was even able to see a new aspect of dating life. Although I was not interested in dating anyone, as I had a girlfriend, I was refreshed and pleased to see that it wasn't openly frowned upon to date outside of your race. I always believed a person should be with whoever makes them happy and families should accept their family members regardless. At the end of the day, it's about being happy. It should never be about where a person came from or what they look like. It should be about who that person is and who they have the potential to become in life. In high school, I witnessed racial riots breaking out on campus for interracial dating. Seeing this new type of diversity was a breath of fresh air for me.

What was not a breath of fresh air would be the amount of playing time I would accumulate over my freshman year on the basketball team, or should I say lack of playing time. In reality, I just was not ready! I remember checking into my first college basketball game; we were playing Derek Fisher and the University of Arkansas Little Rock Trojans. I checked into the game forgetting to take my warmup pants off. I never lived this one down!

One of the bright spots of the season was having a chance to go back to home state and play against the defending NCAA National Champions, the Arkansas Razorbacks, in a game we didn't come close to winning. I actually played several minutes as Corliss Williamson and the rest of the Hogs quickly made the game no contest, allowing me to play against the team I grew up rooting for.

Looking back at my freshman year college basketball program, I see it filled with DNP-CD. This term means, "Did not play, coaches' decision." It probably would have been best I sat out my freshman year, but I didn't. I did gain some decent playing experience, but I don't think it was enough to waste an entire year of basketball. The simple fact is that I just wasn't good enough. I am the last person to make excuses, but I was young and not mentally ready to compete with some of the guys we had on our roster. I needed to practice and get bigger and stronger, which I would over that next summer. I would never say the year was a total failure, as I did maintain good grades, and the coaches were excited to have me coming back as a sophomore.

The summer in between my freshman and sophomore years of college was not as fun and exciting as some the others I have talked about, but I did have my same summer jobs working on the fish farm along with some funeral home duties. Wesley had now become my stepfather, as he had married my mom, taking on the responsibility of six kids plus the two of his own—something I don't think many men would even fathom doing.

Mrs. Wallace was still up to the random phone calls asking my girlfriend, Sherra, and me to pick up the deceased, except one day when she called me to tell me I had to go by myself to get a body. I had to go alone because her daughter was at work. This is another funny story because I knew I would not be going anywhere alone to pick up a dead body ever! One of my favorite cousins happened to be up in Arkansas from Texas to visit his dad for a few weeks during the summer. We spent lots of time together; he knew I worked for the funeral home, washing cars and things of that sort. The day Mrs. Wallace called me to make the solo trip to Little Rock for the body pickup, I immediately made a plan to have my cousin, who was a couple of years younger than me, take the one-hour ride with me. I called my cousin Rae to see if he was free to help me wash a couple of the funeral home cars. I told him if he helped me, I would give him a few dollars whenever Mrs. Wallace paid me. He agreed.

I pulled up to his dad's house, and he hopped into the hearse, thinking we were headed to the car wash. We began to make our way to the north part of Brinkley, passing one car wash.

Rae asked, "Why didn't you stop at that car wash?"

I told him it was because the other one north of town was better. Next, we approached and passed the second car wash. I say second car wash because we only had two in town.

Rae said, "Is that not the only other car wash in town?"

I told him it was, but I wanted to fill the car up with gas at the Chevron up by the interstate before we washed the car. Rae and I passed the overpass, and I quickly exited onto the interstate before getting to the gas station.

Rae asked, "Hey, man, where are you taking me!"

I responded, "Hey, man, Mrs. Wallace told me I had to go and pick up a dead body in Little Rock, and there ain't no way I'm going at it alone, so you better buckle up, buddy!"

The look on his face was priceless. This day was one to remember. I'll leave it at that and spare the details of the two of us actually transporting the body back to the funeral home. He still reminds me of this day every time we see each other. I didn't go alone to pick up a body that day, and I never went alone.

Also, this coming school year I would not be going back to Shreveport alone, as my girlfriend had enrolled and been accepted to the branch of Louisiana State University located in Shreveport. This was a plan which her mom was totally against, but we convinced her to allow it to happen anyway. I was really looking forward to my second year of college.

The year started off well. Everything was going smoothly until I received the call that my great-grandmother Lula had passed away. At the time, this was the most heartbreaking news I had ever received. My great-grandmother played a major role in my life, as I spent lots of time living with her and my great-grandfather when I was younger and my mom and I weren't exactly seeing eye to eye. My great-grandmother never made it to any of my sports games, but she always listened to them on the radio.

The loss took me back to the times when I had initially begun to drive and was earning my learner's permit to be able to drive with a licensed adult. The two of us would take shopping trips together to Memphis and Little Rock when I was barely tall enough to see over the steering wheel of her Mercury Grand Marquis. Great memories, but certainly not something I was equipped to deal with at that time. I was lucky to have my girlfriend there to support me through that tough time. My sophomore basketball season would for sure be dedicated to my great-grandmother.

During my sophomore season, I earned playing time through hard work and some superior athletic ability. I began to earn the trust of the coaches with my defense and willingness to share the basketball. They never had to run a play for me, as I knew and accepted my role on a team that was comprised of seniors. I didn't start any games that year, but I finished almost all of them. We had a pretty good season that year. I had found my comfort zone on the team through my coaches.

I knew going forward into my next year, I would have a major role on the team as an obvious leader and the leading scorer returning for my junior season. (I had averaged just over seven points a game that season, along with being one of the top rebounders on the team.) I was very excited, and I knew that my junior year would be different. Along with my coaches, the expectations for me and the team would be raised to another level. As I reflect back on those first two years of college, I would say at that point, my life was going just fine! Things were going almost exactly according to plan. I was excited to see what the future had in store, as I was halfway done with college.

CHAPTER SEVEN

Highs and Lows

The second half of my college experience would be filled with highs and lows. The end of my sophomore year would come to an end, and as I'd always done, I would be heading home for the summer. I took a summer job at our local Walmart as a part of the remodeling team. I still worked with my stepfather when he needed me and also did a few funeral home duties over the summer.

But this summer would be somewhat different in that my girlfriend and I had pretty much parted ways. I was for effected at the fact that things didn't end exactly the way I had hoped with my girlfriend. I had to accept and take responsibility for it not working just as much as she did. I made a few last-second efforts to reconcile to no success, but to be honest, it was for the best.

In hindsight, I don't recommend any young person going to college being tied down in a relationship. In my opinion, those years should be used to enjoy the experience and continue to find out who you are as a person.

Her mom was absolutely correct, as she had not totally approved of her coming down so close to be with me. It was a learning lesson, but at the same time, with her not wanting to reconcile, it took my motivation to a whole new level. My mindset was that I would do everything I could to make her regret us breaking up. I would do that by performing well on the basketball court. I can't say that she ever had any regrets in our split, but I had officially become the number-one option on my college basketball team.

The season started with me being named one of the captains of the team, as my coaches wanted to show immediate support for me, further heightening the expectations they had for me. We started the season off with mostly road games. The thing about playing at a small NCAA division-one school was that we were required to go on the road and play what they called "money games." This was when bigger schools would pay us to come and play them with the full expectations of blowing the smaller school, us, out, padding their win-loss record. That was exactly what happened to us during those first ten games. I remember going to play at Oklahoma, New Mexico, and TCU, just to name a few. Even back then, these schools had really good basketball teams. We never had much of a chance in most of these games, but we always fought hard, and I fought even harder as the new team leader.

We finally got a road win before we would be heading home for a few days over the Christmas break to spend time with our families. It was a road win at Rice University. It was a good, hard-fought win that we could build on, as we would be heading into conference play after the break and into a more level playing field. During the first two years of my college career, our team had always been middle of the pack in our conference. Things wouldn't be much different this year, but I did continue to put up impressive numbers as the season progressed.

One night, as we played against our conference in-state rival at the time, SE Louisiana in Hammond, Louisiana, I would have the game of my career. I scored a career-high forty-one points and we got an overtime victory over our rival in this meaningful conference game. This was the most points I had ever scored in a basketball game. I had never scored over thirty-five, even back in high school. After this game, along with the week I had in our other games, I was named player of the week in the state of Louisiana and in our conference. It was the first time I had received any recognition in college. I was excited for this honor, but I was even more excited that we had won all of our games during that week. We would go on to finish our season in the middle of the pack, as we had always.

The difference for me this year was that I had a great year statistically. I finished the year with an average of nineteen points and seven rebounds per game. I was also at the top of our league in steals when the season ended. At the conference tournament's year-end banquet, I was named first team all-conference as a result of the season I had, along with leading the conference in scoring that season. The honors were great, and I was extremely excited, but I really wished we had won more games. I was always a guy who put winning first. I was looking forward to the next season, as I felt we had a really good team coming back, and I would have even higher expectations from myself as the leader of the team.

Along with the accolades on the court, I was named student athlete of the year at my school. For me, this was even more important than the things I had done on the basketball court. My high school coach always stressed the importance of cashing in on the free education I was receiving. I was as focused to finish college as I was to excel on the basketball court.

This was also a good year for me in that I had come out of my shell socially, beginning to make more friends and enjoying some of the other aspects of college life. This was a school year that saw me do some dating as well, experiencing some of the things Coach Williams had told me to wait for even back in high school. I began to go out with new friends and party with the frats. My school was really small, so the frats were always happy to see us basketball players out and about, partaking in their weekend parties. It was a lot of fun. I feel it all happened just as planned. I had taken my time to experience these things, therefore I was better able to control myself and some of the decisions that came along with college lifestyle. It was good, responsible fun.

Things were going really well for me, and I was having the time of my life. Basketball and my social life were going well. Just when I was peaking as a person and a player, my teammates and I got the news that our school had decided to move in another direction with the coaching staff. This caught me totally off guard. It felt like a slap in the face. Centenary was not a school that was known for firing any coaches. The news said that Coach had resigned, but he made sure we knew he had not resigned. He met with us, telling us that he had been fired. He spoke of the tough schedule we were forced to play, noting that if he would have known his job was on the line, he would have scheduled more realistically. Regardless, the school was in search of a new coach immediately. I can honestly say I was not excited about the firing, as I had built a three-year rap-

60

port with the staff. The last thing I needed heading into my senior campaign was a new coach. This was the first time in my life that I realized sports really were a business and the first time I began to understand that when it comes to sports, you should always be prepared for the unexpected.

Nonetheless, we would see several coaches come in for interviews over the following weeks. All of the candidates were great. When the decision was made to hire first-time head coach Billy Kennedy, I knew it was important for me to move forward and refocus on adapting to whatever the new staff needed from me. As the leading returning scorer and captain of the team, it was important that I make the transition for the new staff as seamless as possible. I was worried about having to gain trust of a new coaching staff in my final year, but at the same time, I was prepared for the challenge. Heading into my final year of playing college basketball, my expectations were at an all-time high, regardless of who would be coaching me. As an athlete, I knew it was always important to be coachable. I knew I was coachable, and I was focused on not letting anything get in the way of my accomplishing my dreams, which were now dreams of playing professional basketball after my college career.

This goal seemed more realistic as ever as the season began to creep up on us. In the conference media outlets and all the preseason magazines I was handed all of the conference awards based on expectations for me on the coming season. In the magazines, I was named preseason player of the year as well as being named the top NBA prospect in the conference for the coming year. The idea that I was an NBA prospect was crazy to me. Could it really be? I guessed it was, since that's what the magazines stated. I was excited to get the season started, to say the least.

It wasn't very long after the first few practices of the year that I realized I probably would not be having the same season I'd had previously. It was different. The coaching was really good, but it was a totally different style of basketball for me. All of my life, I had played up-tempo, fast-paced basketball. The new coaching staff had a different idea when it came to style of play. I remember our new coach saying that we would not be going on the road getting blown out by these bigger schools. He said if we were to lose games, the scores would be in the fifties as opposed to the one hundreds. It made total since, but I felt even after just a few of the practices that I was not able to take full advantage of my athletic ability as I had done all of my previous basketball-playing years.

As the season began and we began to roll through the schedule, things were going good but not great for me. We were still just an average team. We weren't winning any more games than I had during the first part of my career. Not only were we not any more successful than in the past in regards to winning, but I was not having the season I had anticipated. If we'd been winning games, I'm sure it would not have bothered me as much as it did. We would end the season the same way all of my college basketball seasons ended: average and middle of the pack in conference play. My scoring average would drop that season from nineteen points per game to sixteen. Not only would I not be player of the year in our conference, but I wouldn't even make first team all-conference. One of the freshmen that came in that year and I would both be named second team all-conference. The freshman I played with that year would eventually, by the end of his career, become the second all-time leading scorer in school history! He was a really good player.

I didn't enjoy playing my senior year the way I had years before, but even back then, I felt that everything happened for a reason. Those reasons led me to where I am today, and what happened after the season eventually set me up for what was next in store for me.

About a week after the season was over, I went into Coach's office to enquire about if he thought he could get me into the college slam dunk contest that I had grown up watching every year during NCAA final four weekend on ESPN. He immediately got on the phone and made a couple of calls. The next day, he contacted me about getting together with our student assistant in putting together a short highlight tape of me doing some slam dunking. Our team's student assistant and I jumped right on the video. We went into the empty gym, and he took video of me doing my most impressive dunks. By the end of the day, we had a tape ready to send in for the competition.

A few days after sending the video to the sponsors, I was selected to take part in the slam dunk contest that would be held at the 1998 Final Four just down the road in San Antonio, Texas. I arrived in San Antonio fully expecting to win the competition. I was the shortest contestant in the competition standing at six feet three inches and easily the contestant from the smallest school. I was supremely confident in my ability, and I knew there was not a better college dunker in the country than me, besides Vince Carter. I didn't have to worry about him since he was a junior and they were also playing in the final four.

I would go on to win the slam dunk contest on ESPN that year. It was my biggest sports accomplishment at that time. I was able to represent my college and my hometown on one of the biggest national stages. Many of my college friends tell me it was the most exciting day in the history of my school as well as in my hometown of Brinkley. Classes at my school were cancelled the following day, as the students had partied well into the next morning. I would be given a day in my hometown in honor of winning the event. I was beyond grateful for all the recognition I was getting from winning the contest. It was all great, but I still had bigger dreams—those of playing professional basketball.

This would be a dream I would have to put on hold. By me not having the best senior year along with the NBA having a lockout following the 1998 basketball season, I would not have any real chances to try out at any NBA camps. The lockout along with me still having a semester of school to complete would make it easy for me to turn down a couple of offers overseas to play professionally. My mindset was that if I was not going to play in the NBA anytime soon, then it would be in my best interest to finish my degree while I was already in student mode. It also helped that Centenary agreed to financially honor my scholarship as if I were still playing, therefore not making me pay for that final semester in helping me complete my bachelor's degree.

I would go on that semester to complete what I had started four years earlier. I had completed the necessary requirements

64

to earn my bachelor's degree. This was one thing that I knew could never be taken away from me regardless if I was playing professional basketball or not. As the semester ended, I had one offer on the table to go play basketball in South Dakota that ended up not coming to fruition, so I was left with real life and the necessity to find a job.

I would eventually take a job as a personal trainer at the start of that new year. It was a job I really liked, but a job I knew I wanted to make temporary, as I felt I still had plenty to offer to the game of basketball. Being a personal trainer was a good first post-college job for me. I had moved into an apartment with two of my good college friends. One was a former college basketball teammate of mine, Reggie Love, who had helped me get the job as a trainer, and the other was my friend and former soccer player at Centenary, Allen Sihatrai. We were living the life together. Three single guys working at living.

One day after work, I got home and Allen approached me with a Harlem Globetrotter program; he had attended their performance that night at Centenary as I was working. He opened the program, which was filled with photos and fresh autographs. I asked him what he expected me to do with that. He flipped the program over to the back and showed me a telephone number. He said to me, "I went to their game tonight, and I am sure you can learn to do all of the things they do." I asked him how he got the number. He told me that after the show, during the autograph session, he approached one of the coaches and enquired about information on how to become a member of the team. He said the coach looked at him funny. My friend is a five-foot-six-inch Asian kid who didn't really fit the profile of a typical Globetrotter. He said after a short giggle, he mentioned to the coach that he was asking not for him, but his friend who had won the college dunk contest the previous year. That was how he got the number—he was asking for me.

After I browsed through the program for a couple of minutes, I handed it back to him, giggling and telling him to get that thing out of my face. I wasn't interested in being a Globetrotter. I was a real basketball player with no basketball tricks to mention.

A week or so passed, and after a not-so-great day of work at the gym, I asked if he still had the program. He handed it to me, and the next day, I called to enquire about any opportunities they might have for me as a player. I spoke with one of the head scouts of the team. He told me to send over a highlight tape of me in action and they would have a look. Within a day of sending the highlight tape, he told me they would put me down to attend their annual training camp, which would be coming up in August later in the year. This was about four months down the road, as it was late April when this conversation occurred.

During this four-month stretch, I continued to work and I continued playing local league basketball on a team with some buddies and former college teammates. I really missed the game of basketball, and this was a way for me to stay close to the game and stay in shape. During that four-month stretch, I also sent more highlight tapes out to overseas teams and any basketball organizations that might be interested. As the month of August approached and I continued to play basketball, I would suffer a serious ankle injury at the worst time. The injury was nothing like I had ever experienced. I was just playing for the love of the game and had not even thought of the

Globetrotters. I had even forgot I sent them the video. Ironically, within a week of the ankle injury, the Globetrotters called. They were calling to confirm I would still be interested in attending the camp. I accepted the invite despite the ankle injury. How could I say no? This would be my first time having a professional tryout, and I was determined to make the most of it regardless of any injury. I went to my supervisor at work after accepting the camp invite to inform her of my plans. I was a bit cocky in telling her that she could go ahead and hire someone to take my position, as I would not need the job anymore since I was confident in making the team.

Was this my destiny? I began to wonder if all the things I had been faced with in the previous two years was leading me to meet my destiny. The ups and downs. The highs and the lows. Would it be again me making the most of an opportunity due the simple fact that someone had spoken up and had confidence in my ability? In this case, it was my friend Allen. I had no idea what it all meant going forward, but I knew I had to take advantage of the opportunity. I was ready to give everything I had to start a journey with a team I had never even imagined being a part of. Let's go!

CHAPTER EIGHT

"Hey, Buddy"

It was August of 1999, and the day had come for me to take flight to the annual official basketball training camp of the Harlem Globetrotters. "Take flight" would become literal before all was said and done. One of the first things I learned about the team before I ever left home was that I would not be traveling to New York for any training with the Globetrotters. In fact, I would be flying into Phoenix, Arizona, the actual headquarters of the team at that time. Once landing in Phoenix, I was to be picked up then taken into the mountains of Prescott, Arizona, where the actual camp was to be held. That's right! Many people, including myself, might not have known, but the team was never from Harlem or anywhere near New York. The team had actually been started and founded in Chicago, Illinois. I'll spare you the history details on that for now, as you can google or visit the team's website to get up to speed on all of that great history.

Upon the arrival into training camp, we pulled up to a beautiful hotel that was placed atop what seemed to be the highest point of the quiet town of Prescott. It was breathtaking for me, as I had been a few places in my life but never really anywhere that reminded me of this. I checked into the hotel and was given a folder with the schedule for the next couple of days. There were about twenty guys who had been invited to the start of training camp. I had never heard of any of these guys in my life. We were each assigned to a roommate and understood that we would be practicing twice a day for the next few days.

Participating in a real basketball practice was something I had not actually done in about eighteen months, so I mentally had to reset my mind to prepare for what was in store. The first thing imagined would be that practice would not be a typical basketball practice since it was the Harlem Globetrotters. I imagined we would just be learning to spin basketballs and running figure eights around one another. I was in for an immediate rude awakening!

Once we arrived at the gym, it was time to stretch and get ready. We began with the normal stretching, followed by full court layup drills and shooting. After these drills, they split us up into teams. It was time to scrimmage. I remind you I was dealing with an ankle injury I suffered just a few weeks prior. My ankle was killing me, but I knew this could be my one and only shot at playing professional basketball. It was easy for me to put mind over matter. I was able to perform very well in those first couple of practices. I was playing good basketball, and I felt as if I were jumping higher than I had ever jumped in my life. I think it was a combination of determination, adrenaline, and hunger that allowed me to play at the level I was playing. I remember during this time reflecting on all of the hustle and hard work I had put in even as far back as that summer of eighth grade when I was able to win all of the camp awards. It's difficult to teach hustle and heart. I knew I had both.

Eventually, after the first day of practices, we headed back to the hotel. Upon arriving back to the hotel, we were instructed not to head to dinner for at least thirty minutes because there were to be some phone calls made to the certain rooms. After the thirty minutes, we were free to head down to dinner. That first night, my roommate and I didn't get any phone call, so we were free to move around.

The next morning would be interesting as we loaded up on the vans for the second day of practices. We walked into the gym as we had the previous day and prepared to stretch and get ready to practice. It wasn't hard to notice that about five of the original twenty guys were not present and apparently no longer with us at the camp. Those phone calls after practice had turned out to be cut calls. They had cut five guys after the first day of practice. This idea certainly sent an entirely different type of adrenaline through my body. This was real! This was real professional basketball, and it was every man for himself. I knew I had to be better than I was the day before since I had no aspirations of being on the receiving end of any cut call. On that second day, I was again determined to impress by hustling harder and jumping even higher than the previous day. I didn't think it was possible, but I felt I was indeed jumping higher regardless of the pain in my ankle. I felt it was another good day of practices for me.

Two days of practice had passed, and we had not come remotely close to practicing anything I knew this world-renowned team was famous for. Again, as the practice day ended, we were instructed to once again stay by the phone for at least thirty minutes once we arrived at our hotel rooms. For the second night, the thirty minutes passed, and my roommate and I were in the clear for dinner, apparently surviving the second day of cuts.

Day three of camp had arrived, and we all knew that there had probably been a few more guys sent home. Once we got into stretching positions, we noticed that we were now down to twelve players; we had no idea exactly how many of us would be kept in the end. I just knew I had to go out, play hard, and control what I could, and that was me giving everything I had. The practice on the third day became a little harder, as we didn't have as much time to rest in between scrimmage and drills since we had already lost eight guys. Regardless of how many guys we had left, the practices were even more intense than the days before, as we all knew what was on the line. We all knew if we didn't prove ourselves worthy, we would be heading home. The third day of practice ended the same as the previous, with a meeting at center court. We were informed that the veteran returning Globetrotter players would be arriving for the rest of camp on what would be tomorrow. We were again to sit by the phone for at least thirty minutes upon arrival to the hotel.

My roommate and I again got to the room, waiting to see if we would be receiving a call. Just as we thought, the thirty minutes had passed, and we were preparing to head down to dinner when the phone rang. He looked at me, and I looked at him. Neither one of us wanted to answer the phone. The phone stopped ringing for about fifteen seconds; then it began to ring again. Finally, I agreed to answer the phone. On the other end of that phone call was one of the coaches—the coach who had been with the team longer than anyone in the organization:

Coach Charles "Tex" Harrison. My heart dropped as I answered with a trembling hello. For as long as I live, I will never forget the words that came from his mouth. He said, "Is this Anthony?" That was the name of my roommate. I said, "No, sir!" He said to me, "Then I don't need to speak with you. You can head down to dinner." I said to my roommate, "Hey, buddy, it's for you." At that point, I immediately made my way down to dinner. A dinner which I could barely eat, as I was so nervous that our phone had actually rung that night. I had known upon that call there was a fifty/fifty chance it was for me, but it wasn't.

I eventually made my way back to the room, where my roommate sat on his bed. He was, of course, disappointed at the news he had just received, not even making it down to dinner. He gave me the details of the phone call, sharing with me that they could possibly get him a tryout with the team that the Globetrotters faced when touring. I offered my sympathy and condolences to him that night, but that next morning would be the last time I would ever see him.

That next day would be the day I would meet many of the guys who would set the tone example of what I wanted to be for many years to come.

CHAPTER NINE

A Whole New World

With the arrival of the veteran Globetrotters, it felt like camp had finally begun. The vibe was totally different than what I had experienced those first three nights. These guys came in with such great attitudes and amazingly huge personalities. Of the two things just mentioned, I knew I had at least the great attitude part down, but I would have to work on having more of an outgoing personality if I was to be a part of this team. The practices were still hard, but in a way that was fun to where you didn't even realize how hard you may have been going.

The morning practices would be all competitive with intense scrimmaging—the same as when I had first arrived. But the second practices of the day were set aside to work on learning and practicing skills that the Globetrotters were famous for. We worked on things like the three-man weave, tricky passes, spinning the ball, and the exact science of how to spin the ball. I came to camp not knowing how to do any tricks with the basketball, but I was eager to learn. The three-man weave was pretty easy for me to pick up, as I was always pretty good on my feet as far as having rhythm and being a pretty good dancer.

Over the next ten days, I would have the time of my life learning from the coaches and veteran players about the legacy of the organization and the things it would take to have a long career as a member of the team.

Each and every night after practices and dinner, I would head into the jacuzzi not only to help my body recover, but to get knowledge from these great athletes who were now my teammates. Once the veteran players arrived, there were no more after-practice cut phone calls. We could shower, head to dinner, or do whatever we needed to prepare for practice the next day. There were sixteen returning players and eight rookies present at camp. It was awesome, to say the least. They held daily seminars throughout camp which we were required to attend on subjects such as media training, history of the organization, and finance. One of my favorite days of the camp was photo day. It was the first time I was ever part of a photo shoot. There were professional photographers and makeup artists there to make sure we looked our best for the media program and other promotional photos and videos to be taken that day. Things seemed to be coming full circle again.

That same program my roommate had presented to me five months prior could now possibly have my images. This would be the case once I signed the contract the day before we all departed training camp. It was my first time ever signing a contract. To be honest, I didn't even read the contract. I just signed it. Knowing what I know now and the things life has taught me, I would advise anyone to always have your contract or contracts looked over, as the Globetrotters advised us to do. I was young, and the one thing I did know is that I would be making more than the seven dollars per hour I was making working forty hours per week at the gym as a personal trainer. It wasn't really about the money. It was about me fulfilling a lifelong dream of playing a game I love for pay.

I was excited to get back home and share the news that I was one of the newest members of the Harlem Globetrotters. I recall vividly the day camp broke and I was on the way to the airport to go home. The referee who drove me back to the airport told me that if I kept doing what I did at training camp, I would be a Globetrotter for a long time. He had been with the organization for many years, so he certainly was one to take these wise words from. This stuck with me, making me even more excited about the opportunity I'd been presented with.

I was excited to share with friends and family that they now had a friend and family member who was being called "Flight Time." It was all good and exciting news for me. I say for me because my girlfriend at the time was not quite as excited as I was about making the team. This was pretty evident as soon as I made it back home. She felt that we were doing just fine and that the job of traveling the world would break us apart. She continued to support me, but eventually, she was right. She was happy that I was now presented with the opportunity to make a living doing something I really loved.

Once I got back home, I worked on ball handing and trying to master spinning the ball on my finger. I had to be ready for my first assignment, which would be coming up about a month after I had returned home from camp. I worked so hard to learn to spin the ball on my finger that I eventually burned my fingernail and the tip of my finger to where it wasn't the same for a long time.

The first tour for me was to be a ten-day tour making stops in Belgium, France, and ending in Germany. I didn't know a lot about any of these countries. I had studied some French in high school as well as in college. I immediately wished I had paid a little more attention in my French classes. The things I knew about Germany were things I'd learned in a summer school college Holocaust course I had taken. As for Belgium, I didn't know anything. Research on Belgium would reveal to me it was where the French fry had originated. I would not have imagined that. It was the tip of the iceberg of useless facts I would become knowledgeable of on this new journey of mine. I was ready to go! My passport had been processed, and after a month of patiently waiting, I was on my way to a whole new world!

The day we left the States was full of firsts for me. It was my first time in New York City, being that's where all of the players assigned to that tour would meet up before taking the seven-hour flight to Belgium. It was the first time I had been in an airport lounge. It would be the longest flight I had been on and the first time I was on an airplane with television screens in all of the head rests. I was excited for all of these experiences, and we had not even played a game yet!

Seven hours later, we would land in Belgium. I could immediately feel a sense of being in a place I had never been before. Just walking through the airport, passing through passport control, the smell and vibe was so different than anything I had imagined. I'm not saying it was a bad thing, but it was for sure different. We would eventually retrieve our belongings, making our way to the team buses outside of the Brussels airport.

One of the first things I noticed was how small some of the cars were as we exited the airport. For the first time, I saw a car that was labeled and named a smart car. I remind you, this was 1999. The first thing I thought was, *These cars will never make it to the States.* We all know how that turned out. The cars were in a display that looked like something you would see on a cartoon. They were stacked up about five building floors, and the display was turning in circles to make sure you could get a full view of the miniature car. The size of this car blew my mind, but I would eventually get past that.

We arrived at the hotel about a half hour later, and we were lodged right in the center of Brussels. It was so lively and festive. People were just hanging out and lounging all around the area. The only time I had ever seen so many people in one area on bicycles was when I would watch highlights of the Tour de France on ESPN. Where was I? What world had I fallen into? Certainly not one I was used to, but at no time was I not excited to see more of what Europe had to offer.

One thing I had not thought about before flying to Europe was the food situation. Much to my surprise, I wouldn't have to look very far. McDonald's was just as popular in Europe as it was in the States. Most of the guys on my first tour didn't really venture out to try other foods. We spent most of that tour eating McDonald's, Pizza Hut, and the popular European fast food restaurant called Quick. Quick, in my opinion, is just a European version of McDonald's. The food situation for the most part was fine. If any of us had missed home at all, there was nothing like the McRoyal (quarter-pounder with cheese) to bring us back!

After being in Europe for just a couple of days, I certainly was not ready to leave or go back home anytime soon. It was time for our first show, which would be my first time even attending a Globetrotter event. My first Globetrotter game would not be as a spectator; it would be as an actual Harlem Globetrotter.

Over the course of the first day and a half, several practices had taken place in preparation for the show. One of the things I couldn't figure out was how we were going to reach the fans during the game being that it seemed most of them didn't even speak English. The first game started, and I was immediately in shock, as our veteran showman "Showtime" Gaffney was using words I had never heard before. I asked our legendary coach "Geese" Ausbie what he was saying. To my surprise, "Showtime" had the ability to speak a little Flemish and French, a gesture you could immediately tell the fans appreciated as they laughed at every word he spoke or attempted to speak in their language. I found myself laughing as well just from seeing the reaction of the audience. Before I knew it, my time had come. It was time for me to check into the game.

This was my first time checking into the game as a Globetrotter. The check-in was much smoother than my first time checking into the game as a college player, as I actually removed my warmups this time before stepping on the court. On the other hand, I had never been more nervous in my life! The laughing went to nervousness and fear. Within the first two minutes, I had managed to shoot an airball and miss a dunk. I was shell-shocked. My first thoughts were that Coach would be calling my room when we got back to the hotel to inform me that I was cut. This was not a good feeling.

80

Once the first half ended, we made our way to the locker room. I knew I had not played well, but I felt everyone else was doing just fine. Turned out I was wrong. Apparently, none of us were performing up to Globetrotter standards. The captain of the team at that time, Clyde "The Glide" Sinclair, ripped into all of us, demanding more and laying the foundation in our brains about the pride and effort it takes to be a Globetrotter. I remember him telling us the team had been around for over seventy years and it was our responsibility to make sure we continued that tradition for the new generation of Globetrotters. This was something that would never leave me though out my entire career. We had a responsibility for two hours each night regardless of what life threw us off the court to make sure the iconic brand that is the Harlem Globetrotters was carried on at the highest level.

The second half was much better than the first half of the show. I immediately noticed exactly what he meant. All of the guys on the tour took their energy to another level for that second half. I remember after the game Coach asking me if I had a good time. I told him I had the best time ever, and I promised him that I would work hard in becoming one of the best Globetrotters ever. He smiled and said, "I know you had a good time. You were laughing so hard at one point that I almost sent you to the ticket window to purchase yourself a ticket!" He was absolutely right. I should have had to buy a ticket, but I didn't have to because I had earned my way in becoming a part of history. I was a part of the most popular basketball team in the world. I felt this immediately and throughout the duration of this tour.

Throughout this tour, my play picked up and I continued to be amazed by the level at which my veteran teammates performed. I continued to be amazed by how our master showman changed his language during the show as we made our way through France and Germany. I was even able to give him a few French words since I had studied it for a few years during school. This tour would turn out to be a great success for me. I was with an awesome group of guys who helped me and allowed me to learn from them. I'm sure our team captain, "Glide," got tired of me really quickly, as I would follow him all over the arenas, trying to get him to help me learn how to handle the ball and do the tricks he was able to do. He never once turned me away. Help from guys like him prepared me very well for what was in store during the States tour, or what we called the domestic tour.

The domestic tour was what I called the "long haul." We were to leave home five days before Christmas, not returning home until mid to late April if you were not assigned to the seven-week European tour that immediately followed the domestic tour. The start of the domestic tour when I first joined would kick off in Orlando at Disney's Wide World of Sports. I had never been to Disney before, so I had no issue at all missing Christmas with my family. I always felt fortunate and blessed to be in a situation that I knew many people had worked so hard to achieve and would never achieve. I was experiencing things that people save and some spend life savings to experience. It would be selfish of me to think any other way.

Once the tour kicked off, I was ready for any challenge or assignment they wanted to give me. I had improved my ball handling over the break to a point where I was nearly as good as some of the second- and third-year players. My plan was for my Globetrotter experience to become a career instead of a job. That was what drove me. That first tour seemed to fly by. I had so many awesome experiences and learned so much during those four months on the domestic tour. I had an opportunity to be a part of a major film in Hollywood called *Little Nicky* starring the great Adam Sandler. It was all just a total out-of-body experience for me. I was able to play in front of all of my friends and family across the United States from Arkansas, Illinois, Tennessee, and Illinois, to name a few.

Within that first tour, I had traveled to nearly thirty states. Before joining the Globetrotters, I had only been to about ten states. I was living a real-life dream. I was seeing things I could not have imagined, and because of my hard work and continued improvement, I was selected to go back to Europe for the seven-week European tour that would cover ten countries.

This tour would start in Sweden and Denmark. Sweden and Denmark were two more places I, of course, had never been. I had also never been on tour with our longest-standing Coach Harrison. Coach Harrison had been with the organization for around fifty years and was also the coach who, back in training camp, had made the cut calls. He was known to be very outspoken and fun. He could make or break any player on the team with just a few words. The other thing about him was that if you got on his good side, then you had nothing to worry about. I had to make sure I got on his good side.

I was a bit of a last-minute addition to the tour. I had taken on a stronger role on the team as the last month of the domestic tour ended. I was a dunker, I was a decent dribbler, and I also opened the show with a solo act of trick shots and juggling. Being that I was a first-year player, Coach was not convinced I could handle this role, so the first thing he did once we started our first practice in Sweden was to roll me three basketballs. He said, "They say you can do this shit, so let me see what you can do!" I was terrified. I tried to juggle, and the balls were going all over the court. I tried to execute my part in the traditional magic circle that we did as a team before every game, and I sucked at that. I tried my trick shots, and none of them would go into the basket. He was immediately convinced that I was not ready and people had been lying to him about what I had been doing on the domestic tour. Following this horrible display, one of my teammates we called "Smokey" came to me in a rage. "Smokey" had taken me under his wings and was like a big brother to me already. He had been on every tour with me to this point, and he knew what I could do. "Smokey" said, "Man, F him and do what you do!" It was exactly what I had needed to hear at that time.

I grabbed the basketballs and began to show Coach that I actually could do the things he had been hearing about. It took a second try, but he had now seen that I could handle my role. I could be a big part of making that seven-week tour a success. All it took was a few encouraging words from a veteran teammate who had confidence in me, knowing what he had seen and what I was capable of.

The first games in Sweden were absolutely packed! We had a double-header on the very first day of the tour. We performed in the Globe Arena in Stockholm. Sixteen thousand fans for both shows, and I'm proud to say I literally didn't drop the ball. I showed Coach that he could count on me. Over the course of the tour, much to his surprise, I had his confidence and support. I mixed that up with playing cards with him daily, something he thoroughly enjoyed doing, and I really had no worries at that time.

Over the course of this European tour, I would experience much more than I had on my first trip traveling over the Atlantic Ocean. For the first time in my life, I realized that if I had to, I could live in other parts of the world. I learned that I had the capability to adjust to anything thrown at me. I enjoyed everything about that tour, from the long bus rides on some days to the late nights in France when I realized after the shows that there was nowhere to eat because everything was closed. The nightlife experiences were fun and very different compared to what I had been used to. I learned that you could fall in "like" with girls you could barely communicate with. I use like instead of love. I do believe there is a difference. Regardless, I knew my horizons had been broadened and I was seeing the world in a totally different lens.

After seven weeks, the tour would come to an end. Although I was having a great time, I was pleased to be heading home from this new world and back to my normal world. I was excited to get back and share my experiences with my friends and family. They were just as excited for the chance to hear about the experiences. Along with being enthusiastic in sharing my stories, I was also looking forward to the potential for what could be next with the team for me and the opportunity to make more memories as well as a chance to continue my hard work on my new craft which had allotted me these dream experiences. How did I get here? More importantly, how would I stay here?

★ CHAPTER TEN

Patience, Kindness, and Real Life

Over the next six to seven years, many things would happen in my life. In a few cases, my patience and kindness would be tested. Anyone who really knows me knows that my motto is "Patience and kindness." No matter what I may be dealing with in life, I never waver from this motto because it is a staple for my way of thinking. I would also be handed some real-life situations over this time, several of which I will talk briefly about throughout this chapter. I will start with my second training camp.

The second training camp for me was pretty interesting. The good thing for me this time around is that I didn't have to come to camp early since I was no longer a rookie. I was now a second-year player and a reliable person to the team. Upon my arrival to camp, it didn't take long for me to realize I was the only returning player from the eight rookies who had been signed from my first training camp. It was evident that the turnover rate was pretty high, and it was important to continue the process of becoming a Globetrotter. True veterans stressed that this would be a process that takes several years to fully complete, but I was game for the challenge.

Along with becoming more charismatic and fun during the early stages of my career, it was also important to continue to be the best basketball player I could be. The great Mannie Jackson was the team owner during the early years of my career. He was a former all-American at the University of Illinois as well as a former Harlem Globetrotter. Mr. Jackson was the first African American in the States to have sole ownership of a major American sports franchise. Mannie was a great businessman, but the thing that I think excited him the most in owning the team was his passion for competitive basketball. This was easy to understand since he was such a good basketball player during his time at the University of Illinois. He wanted the Globetrotters not only to be the best family entertainment in the world, but also one of the best basketball teams in the world. This was evident in training camps and practices.

While attending my second training camp, there were guys who I had actually heard of and guys I had idolized as a kid. There were guys who had excelled even in the NBA. I was certainly in awe of many of these guys, but at the same time, I realized we were all competing for jobs with the team. I knew regardless of how skilled they had been in the past that I was hungrier than they were to have a long career with the Globetrotters. This was obvious, as some of these guys eventually only used the opportunity as a quick stop and others as a stepping stone, so to speak, to whatever was next on the back end of their careers. For me, the mindset was to step into every level of what it would take for me to have a long career with this brand, which I had fallen in love with so quickly. From listening and being attentive to the veteran players who had made careers out of their opportunity, I knew what it would take. These were the guys I would follow. These were the guys I would allow to lead me instead of the passersby no matter how much I might have admired them in my youth. I was a part of something big, and I knew it. I knew the brand was all about family and had a zero tolerance for anything that would interrupt that, which was one of many brand promises. There were guys who didn't understand that.

That was obvious during this second training camp. About a week into the two-week training camp, we walked into the gym just like the other days. But on this particular day, things would be different. We walked into the gym and were instructed to drop our practice duffle bags in the bleachers and to head into the auxiliary gym next door. We were not allowed to enter this gym with any of our belongings, as the athletic trainers kept a close eye on everyone.

When we entered the building, there were several stations set up, but not the stations you would expect in a gym. The gym was set up for random drug testing. This was not something I was worried about, as I am not a drug user, but I could see that a few guys appeared to be a bit worried. Several guys were obviously in shock. We had all taken drug tests in the physicals we took before training camp, but apparently, something had happened at camp that had raised someone's level of curiosity. No one had expected this. As a kid, I had seen the negative effects of using banned substances. I just never got into it, and I knew it was never worth my job. That day of random drug testing did just that: it cost several players their jobs. The owners made a point that day, that in order to be a part of the organization, you had to make sacrifices. Family entertainment and over seventy years of history did not mix with banned substances. You didn't have to tell me this twice. The point had been made.

Over the course of the years that followed, there would be random drug test during tours. More guys than I would have expected would be out of a job as a result of these not-so-smart decisions. I would not be one of those, as I made a promise to myself and to the organization that I could be counted on.

Mannie showed me he had faith in me that second year, giving me a bonus that I really needed but didn't expect. The bonus allowed me to get my head back above water, as I still had some outstanding balances on a couple of credit cards I had accumulated over my college career. That seven-dollar-an-hour job at the gym as a trainer just didn't help with that. With the bonus, I was able to pay off those debts and begin to restore my credit. As a freshman in college, the credit card companies got me with the free t-shirts and things of that sort just to sign up. How the heck was I getting credit cards with no job? I don't know, but they gave them to me, and it was hard not to use them at times. I advise any college kid to be careful with credit cards and what the misuse of them can do to your future. I could give a class on that! Nevertheless, I got myself to zero and was now on the way up.

Even after receiving the helpful bonus, I continued to live as if I were working as a trainer making seven dollars per hour. I still had my same 1991 Dodge Dynasty I went to college in as a freshman. The only thing that changed that year is I purchased my first cell phone. I always wanted a cell phone. I purchased a plan that allowed one thousand talk minutes for a pricey $150 per month. There was no texting!

Also, my good friend Allen and I moved into a two-bed-room apartment, and life was good. Allen was the friend I mentioned who had attended the Globetrotter game and in-spired me to try out. The two of us living together was a great deal for him. We would split the bills, and I would be gone half the year, but when I was there, we would have so much fun!

We had almost as much fun as I did on the tour during this second year. One of the several memories I have from that sec-ond year would be a visit to South Carolina State House. In looking back, I would not say it was a fun visit, as it was the first time I realized the respect and power the brand of the Harlem Globetrotters had built over its duration. The visit in-cluded about five players and our coach. We spoke with the governor about the controversial confederate flag that was fly-ing over the state house at that time. It was simple from the side of the Globetrotters. Either the flag goes down or we don't play in South Carolina anymore. We were to boycott the state, and this would actually happen. As an organization, the team would not return to South Carolina for about fifteen years after that tour. This was something that was bigger than me, but an eye-opening experience for sure. I liked South Carolina and was a bit sad not to be playing there for the years we passed the state by.

Over the next couple of years, with the team, things seemed to be a bit stagnant. Besides a Jay Leno appearance and filming a Burger King commercial, I didn't feel I was gaining much headway in regard to respect. I loved what I was doing, but I was beginning to not feel the love. I was doing everything that was asked of me from the team, and it seemed I was not being rewarded accordingly. Over the years, a carousel of guys came and went. I don't remember many of them and never even took their phone numbers or emails. Through those years, I knew some of these guys were being paid well for their stops with the team. Why were they being taken care of in a sense and guys like me, who were making themselves an integral part of the organization, seemingly weren't being taken care of accordingly? Guys who were there for all the hard work and practices.

I didn't understand it, but I knew it had become more than about the money. I felt that if I could just continue working hard, stay patient, and keep a kind heart, things would eventually improve for me as well as my closest teammates/friends. One of my closest friends and teammates who is now a successful head basketball coach at his alma mater would joke of becoming millionaire Globetrotters just like Mannie Jackson. These were always fun conversations. The what-if games. The what-if games led me to one of my craziest years, which was 2005.

2005 would be my sixth year with my dream job as a member of the Globetrotters. I was finally making good money, and the team seemed to be committed to me long term. Then, real life started to come into play. A sequence of events during this year would force me to refocus my life and get myself more together mentally than I had ever been before. The first thing that happened to me was a car accident.

I was allowed to go home for a quick week during the tour of 2005 as a result of my six-year legacy status with the team. I never really cared about going home during the tour, but if they were offering it, I felt I may as well take it. I went home about a month into the domestic tour that year. When I got home, I decided to drive over to Dallas, which was about a

92

three-hour drive away, to catch up with some friends. On my way back to Shreveport the following day, I was involved in a car accident. I remember this accident as clearly as if it happened yesterday.

The day was gloomy, and light rain was coming down before I realized a large Ford F-350 pickup truck had dipped into the interstate median and was headed directly toward me. Before I knew it, I was hit and forced about fifty feet off the interstate. I remember the airbag deploying and glass flying all over me. Once the car stopped, I heard a hiss and realized I was still alive and good. I climbed out of the window and ran away from the vehicle as fast as I could. I collapsed and rolled to my back. Before I knew it, there were several people standing over me. The guy who hit me was openly remorseful, trying to explain that he had been run off the interstate by a speeding eighteen-wheeler. It seemed my life had flashed before my eyes! I was in an ambulance and being told by the paramedic how I was lucky to be alive as we hurried away to the hospital. I was fine. I felt fine. She asked me if I was able to get a glimpse of my vehicle while continuing to tell me how fortunate I was to be alive. I knew I was fortunate. The vehicle was a total loss, and I walked away with nothing more than a couple of scratches and minor bleeding. I was released that night and already eager to get back to tour.

I would return to the tour as scheduled as the week's vacation came to an end. I had a bit of shoulder soreness, which would keep me off the court for a game or two, but I was back before I knew it. On that same tour, just a few weeks after returning to the court, I met the woman who would eventually be the mother of my son Nicholas.

Things were happening super fast! Real life was coming full speed ahead. I was advised by family members to convince her to not have the baby, but this was not something I even thought of doing. I explained to the concerned parties that I was nearing thirty and had no children. I explained how I didn't make it my business going around making babies and how I felt the child was meant to be, much to the chagrin of the main people I had these discussions with. I explained that the child's mother and I had made no promises to each other but that if she wanted to proceed with my child, I would fully support her decision. I began financially supporting my son before I was even sure he was mine.

The summer before my son was born became very stressful for me, as I was dealing with some other issues. My mind seemed to be getting fragile, and I now worried about things I'd never had to worry about. This led me to a situation I am not proud off. My fragile mindset during this time led me to a half of a night in jail.

One night while out on the town with friends, I entered a local night club. My good friend I was with had been given a bit of a hard time getting in, eventually getting him arrested. I had no idea what had actually taken place, as I had already entered the establishment. A few minutes after I entered, I felt a tap on my shoulder by a man who informed me that my friend and his girlfriend had been cuffed and taken to jail. As I was exiting the nightclub, the disagreement that ensued between me and the guy at the door would get me cuffed as well. I couldn't believe it. What had I done? I was headed to bail my friend out, and now I was going as well.

I remember calling my mom that night as part of my one phone call. She cried, "Not my good son." I felt horrible, as I could hear the disappointment in her voice. I was sitting in jail. How had I gotten there? I was the guy who one day a teammate of mine asked, "How can you be so nice to everyone all of the time?" Was I not nice to someone in this instance, or was it just a big misunderstanding? Regardless of what I wondered, the fact of the matter was that I had been arrested and had disappointed my mom. I would get out within a few hours. The charges would be dropped within a day and expunged from my record, but I took responsibility. I took responsibility for my action of not just walking away from the situation.

With all that's happening today with the justice system, I will not say why I think I was arrested, but it was bogus. It was my fault for even allowing myself to be vulnerable in that situation. I just remember asking the officer what I did wrong and him saying to me that I had trespassed on the premises of the club. When I got the rap sheet, it said I had been detained as a result of disorderly conduct. Life had become about as real for me as it had ever been, and it was up to me to let it spiral or regain control.

I chose to gain control. I knew what I needed to do, and I was grateful for the things that caused me to refocus. Training camp of 2005 had come just in time for me to get back in my groove. I signed my best contract to that point of my career while at training camp. The timing could not have been better, being that my son was to be born a few months later.

This would also be the year in which ownership of the team was to transition into the hands of Shamrock Capital, an investment group that would bring in a new company president who would play a major part in taking my career from stagnant to a level I had only imagined during my first six years with the team. I didn't expect this change, as I knew the company was doing well with Mannie at the helm, but I also knew I was okay with change and ready to adapt in whatever way I needed to prolong my career. That's right—it was no longer a job for me. I felt I had a chance to have a long career with the team if I continued to play my cards. My positive way of thinking allowed me to accept that change could be good. Real life had landed on me, but I was excited to see how much further patience and kindness would take me!

CHAPTER ELEVEN

Destined

As the next year or so would unfold, I was able to see some of the changes that would be taking place. For some of us, change would be good, and for others, the result would not be so good, as a few of the veteran players would eventually call it quits. For some of us, it's difficult to accept change. It's especially difficult when you have become so comfortable doing things a certain way for so long. Change was no problem for me. Reinventing was no problem for me.

One of the things my first owner, Mannie, shared with me one day when I visited his home stuck in my head. After my fifth season, he told me the second part of my career would be totally different from the first part. I think what he meant by this was that in sports, as you get older, there will be physical abilities that will diminish, but if you can find a niche, you can overcome the physical deterioration. Him telling me this made me even more determined to learn as much as possible about every part of being a Globetrotter. Mannie had sold a large percentage of the team but still had an influence on some parts of the company as it transitioned.

The transition into the arrival of our new CEO, Kurt Schneider, was very positive not only for me, but for many of the other players that were still a part of the team during the change of ownership. Kurt arrived in May of 2007. The positive energy and excitement he could spread through a room was infectious; his arrival was almost as exciting as the birth of my second child, Reya, that same year.

Nonetheless, Shamrock and Kurt came in with the mindset to create stars. This was a concept that had been pushed aside since after the days of the most popular Globetrotter legends of the 1970s and 1980s, when the team was at the climax of its popularity. Over the course of many years, it had become more about the brand as opposed to creating stars. Shamrock and Kurt came in with what I would call a Hollywood mindset. Kurt had come to us via WWE, where he had worked for many years under the tutelage of Vince McMahon. The plan was to bring the team back to the popularity of the 1970s and 1980s. There were some minor issues happening within the organization during the early transition that compelled Kurt to put nicknames back on the jerseys of the players as well as sell these jerseys in the arenas in which we would be performing. Kurt said he wanted fans to see us more than the one time a year that we would come to local arenas. Kurt wanted people to recognize players outside of the famous red, white, and blue uniforms that the organization had made so iconic and popular. He wanted people to recognize us walking though places like airports and even grocery stores in our regular street clothes. Shamrock and Kurt had the vision of creating the next generation of popular Globetrotters, and our CEO felt with the rise of social media along with television, this is exactly what they could do.

They would start buy bringing people in to work with the organization who had Hollywood ties and backgrounds. Before accepting the job as CEO of the Globetrotters, Kurt had secretly done some scouting of the tours, giving him a pretty good idea of the players he would choose to put in the forefront of the new plans of the organization. Luckily, I was one of those guys he saw the potential in. He and several others who were still a major part of running the organization put this plan in play. I was extremely happy and grateful that through the transition, several of the people who had been with the organization longer than me would still be making major decisions, as I knew they understood me and the hard work I had put in over those early years.

That year in training camp would be very different from any other I had experienced. First off, by the time Shamrock took over, the offices remained in Arizona, but the training camps would now be in New York. It was a nice change of pace from the hills of Arizona. Nothing against Arizona, but I was happy to be training not far from where most people assumed the team had been founded. Having training camp in New York, we would have many more visitors and guests coming to camp daily, sharing knowledge on many things as usual, but also new things such as practicing ad lib. This was a riot of fun. Imagine a room of about thirty players being creative and coming up with things off the cuff. This is no doubt what the team was known for, but it was being taken to a new level.

We were also allowed during one meeting to talk about TV and the shows we either watched or liked the most. The purpose of this was that we would begin to pitch the idea of actually taking part in some of these shows. This idea was right along the lines of the vision Kurt had come in with. I remember guys including myself rattling off the ideas of shows such as *Hell's Kitchen, Survivor, Extreme Makeover Home Edition*, and *The Amazing Race*. We didn't really think we would ever be able to take part in any of these shows, but we all liked the wishful thoughts. Besides the yearly appearances on ABC's *Wide World of Sports*, the Globetrotters had not really been on network television since shows like *Love Boat* and *Gilligan's Island*. We were starting to believe these could be realistic opportunities.

That first year of touring under our new CEO was full of excitement for me and many of my teammates. In that first year, I was informed by the team that I would have to change my jersey number since the number I had been wearing was to be retired. I had no problem with changing number, as it actually belonged to one of the all-time great Globetrotters Fred "Curly" Neal. Curly was always a true idol of mine who I was a fan of even before I became a member of the team. My great-grandmother loved him and the Globetrotters from as far back as I remember. Curly wore the number twenty-two for a total of twenty-two years as a member of the organization and what better honor for him than to have his number retired at Madison Square Garden for his contribution.

It was an honor for me to give up the number and even more of an honor to actually take part in the ceremony that evening at half-time on that day. I was allowed to talk about how humbled I was to have been allowed to share that number for the time it was lent to me. It was a great night and event in which we were able to honor a legend of the game in front of his family and many of the fans who had grown up idolizing him. For as honored as I was to have the number, I was excited to figure out what number I would wear next.

It was decided that over the summer there would be a poll on the team's website which would allow the fans to figure out the number I would wear for the rest of my career. This was exciting for me for the simple fact that I would even be considered worthy of a poll question on the website. The number chosen by the fans was four, which was the same number I'd worn during my college career.

Things were really looking up for me in this first year with the new regime. I was trusted to give an important speech at that retirement ceremony. Additionally, for the first time in eight years, I was one of the players featured on the cover of the yearly Harlem Globetrotter game program—the same program my good friend Allen had presented to me the night he attended that Globetrotter game back in 1999 when I was working making an honest living as a personal trainer. I was now on the cover. It sure felt like destiny to me. Destiny would also take another turn as one of my favorite teammates from early in my career would be allowed to rejoin the team during that following training camp of 2008. His name was Chris Richardson.

Chris was a couple of years younger than I was. He had taken a similar path to me in becoming a Globetrotter. Chris came from a similar background as me, having been raised in a single-parent home in the South as well as having had a pretty good college basketball career. Like myself, Chris had taken part in the college slam dunk contest at the end of his senior year of college at UNLV. When Chris first joined the team a few years after me, I took an immediate liking to him, and we were at times inseparable while on tour. He was like a little brother to me. I was very disappointed when Chris was released from the team, but that same level of disappointment couldn't compare to the excitement I felt to see him back with the team.

Chris was taller than I was and was about as athletic as you could be at six feet seven inches tall. He could jump out of the gym. Chris made such an impression at camp upon his return that he earned the nickname "Flash." It was super fitting for him, as he could get off the floor so quick and dunk in a flash. If you were not paying attention, you would miss it. The same way some people missed the backboards, he would break on tour with his powerful dunks. The backboard he broke while on tour with us in Mexico just a few weeks after we departed training camp remains in my head. Chris was back! He was flying as high as ever with the way he was performing nightly. I was happy and so proud to see my friend getting a second chance to do what I knew he had loved and missed for several years during his layoff. That Mexico tour went great! We had so much fun and were excited to learn that just a few weeks after the Mexico tour, we would be chosen as the group who would entertain the troops during the annual Armed Forces Tour.

For us, this tour was always rewarding, as it gave us an opportunity to bring a bit of home to many troops and their families who are stationed abroad and don't often get the same opportunities as we do for live entertainment. It was always one of my favorite tours, and I was excited to be sharing with not only Chris, but also my other new best buddy, "Big-Easy" Lofton. "Big Easy" had joined us via one of the most interesting routes.

Just the year before, "Big Easy" had led his college team, the Southeastern Louisiana Lions, to the NCAA tournament. This was a school I was extremely familiar with, as I had posted my career against them back in my college days. "Big Easy" was a survivor of Hurricane Katrina. The evacuation that resulted from the hurricane led him to Houston, where, amid the chaos of the hurricane, he would be given a tryout with the Globetrotters. He would make the team and be given his nickname based on being from New Orleans as well as the way he could easily get along with people even though he was at what might seem to be an intimidating six-feet-nine-inches-tall stature. We both played for Coach Billy Kennedy, but at two different colleges, and when "Big Easy" joined the team, Coach called me to make sure I would take him under my wing, a process that was easy and seamless. "Flash," "Easy," and I were labeled by one of the coaches as the "Three Amigos." You didn't see one without the other two. During that Mexico tour, we were attached at the hip, and this would not change once we crossed the Pacific Ocean to embark on the Asia military tour. What would happen halfway through this two-week tour affects to me even today.

On what was a normal day for us on the military base, we would all get up to have team breakfast together. The problem this morning was that one of us was missing—Chris. Maybe he had overslept. One of our other teammates ran back to check up on Chris. Our teammate returned to us, dripping sweat, explaining that the maid had let him into Chris's room and Chris would not wake up. He said Chris was cold and stiff. We all sprinted to the barracks to face the realization that Chris had passed away that night in his sleep. This was easily the most shocking and devastating thing that would happen to me over my eventual eighteen-year career. All of us eventually made our way back home without our brother. Most of us made it to his funeral for one last goodbye. He was taken away so quickly and unexpectedly. Chris was gone, but we knew while he had been back with us that he'd had the time of his life. We all knew and promised ourselves that we would do everything in our power to honor him so his legacy would not be forgotten. That year, we all wore his initials on our uniforms for the duration of the tour.

Some of the things Kurt had envisioned were coming to fruition. During that year, we were starting to appear on some of the shows discussed in the meetings just a couple of years before. Four of us had appeared on the hit show *Hell's Kitchen* at a bar mitzvah. We had some of our guys on *Home Edition Makeover* along with cameos on other top shows such as *The Bachelorette* on ABC. Opportunities were actually becoming reality, and for "Big Easy" and me, no bigger opportunity would come than *The Amazing Race*.

The Amazing Race was always one of my favorite television shows, and after a strenuous process of applying, auditioning, and flying back and forth to Los Angeles, we had been selected to run during season fifteen. We were beyond excited for the opportunity. We were not only excited to run the race for ourselves, but just as equally excited to run the race for our dear friend Chris and his family. The organization had trusted and allowed us to represent the company on one of the biggest stages—a stage which millions of people each and every week would be tuned into.

The thing about being a Globetrotter is that you must take on certain responsibilities that some athletes might shy away from. You must realize and accept being a role model. You have to accept that kids look up to you and realize the importance of displaying yourself in the best light possible for these fans. It's a part of the job of being an ambassador to one of the most popular sports brands in the world. We were accepting of this responsibility, realizing we had a chance to represent over eighty years of entertainment and show the world that the Globetrotters were still around and we were carrying on the role of being just as good a people as the Trotters many grew up idolizing. We wanted to win, of course, but we knew it was important for people to see what we as people and Globetrotters were all about. We wanted to show kids and adults that you can have fun and compete at the same time.

As I look back at the opportunity we had with *The Amazing Race*, I have nothing but great memories. We didn't win the race, but we raced in a way that would have made it difficult for any person not to like us or what we stood for. During the course of the tour that year, we were told numerous times how each and every week, many of these families would sit down and watch the show because they knew they would be able to share teachable moments with their kids and loved ones. We had so many fans come up to us telling us how they were not even basketball fans but had become fans of the Harlem Globetrotters because of the way we represented the brand on the show. These were just a few of the many compliments we received during the tour. These compliments in the way they made us feel were way more valuable than anything we could have gained by winning that race. People would show up to the arenas holding signs with our names on them. It was super exciting.

One thing I remember from the first time we ran the race happened at the Minneapolis airport. "Big Easy" and I were sent to do some promoting together for the upcoming shows that were to take place in Minneapolis during the domestic tour. We were standing at the baggage claim waiting to retrieve our bags when we were first recognized. We were wearing regular street clothes. Kurt's idea had actually come to be reality. The young lady approached us with tears in her eyes, explaining how much she loved us and the way we had raced. It made me really nervous; I remember telling her please not to cry. It was one of the most exciting times of my life, traveling city to city and state to state, interacting with fans of the Harlem Globetrotters and *The Amazing Race*.

Along with this new popularity also came other issues with success and the fifteen-minutes-of-fame TV stardom. Any athlete that becomes a part of a professional team has to deal with family and friends who sometimes come out of the woodwork, so to speak. It is so hard to say no to people at times, especially people who you grew up with and who have been through struggles with you. Over the years, sometimes it seemed some individuals felt a sense of entitlement to the things I had accomplished. It's true that in many cases, we had become successful as a result of drive and push from all facets of people involved in our journey, but I never believed anything monetary should be owed or expected from our supporters. People assumed that seeing us on TV or playing in front of thousands of people each and every night automatically made us rich. This was not always the case.

I had one family member call me once about helping to buy a car. This family member informed me that they had located a car they really liked. I was told that their contribution to the car could be about 10 percent; they hoped I could contribute the rest. I would have loved to do this, but what they did not realize was that I had kids and things I had to take care of as well.

At times, having to ignore and say no to family and friends sent me into some of the deepest depression I could never have imagined. Things started to mess with my head in ways that led me to face a demon I never saw coming: the demon of depression. I quickly began to realize after this couple of successful years that it didn't matter how much I had—I was dealing with things in my mind that I could not control, but for the sake of not appearing selfish, I chose not to ever share my having to deal with depression. Destiny had taken me to success, and destiny had also taken me into occasional sadness that at times I could not control. As long as the good outweighed the bad, I felt I was fine, and I am thankful for the control I did have in bringing myself out of my depression every time. One thing that helped me was work. I was never sad when I was working. During this stretch, most of my depressing times occurred while living alone.

People would often ask if I had ever dreamed of being a part of the organization I played for. I had to be honest. I told them no way! The life I was now living, doing what I loved, was more than a dream come true. I always imagined the big crowds and the fans, but I never imagined these fans would be from all around the world. I had the best job, and I felt I was living my best life. I was just reaching the tip of the iceberg of future opportunities.

CHAPTER TWELVE

Presidents

The months and years that followed these first appearances on some of these top network television shows were followed with ups and downs. Ups and downs that are no different than the ups and downs any individual faces in life. I can say without any doubt that most of mine were ups.

As I mentioned in the last chapter, I began to spend more time alone. Most of the time alone came when I was not touring, as I had moved out of my home and into an apartment, mainly for my own peace of mind. When I say peace of mind, I don't mean the situation I was living in was the worst in the world. My daughter's mom and I had been living together for around three years, and with touring the world most of the year along with having a young daughter, things were not always easy. Road life can be really hard, as any professional athlete or performer can attest to. Any person who spends most of the year away from their family can understand exactly what I mean. My daughter's mom was and is a great person who continues to do an excellent job raising our daughter, but I knew she was more stressed out than she should have been when it came to me. Leaving the situation was not easy, but in the end, we both agreed that it was for the best. I moved out of my house into an apartment, knowing it was more important for my daughter to live better than myself. I didn't really need a nice home since I was gone for most of the year anyway. Her mom and I eventually came to an agreement that worked for us both moving forward. I knew there were things I was dealing with that, in my opinion, needed to be dealt with alone. I always thought I would rather be alone and be down than to bring someone else down with me. Maybe that's not the best way of thinking, but it was my way of thinking.

That year, I was dealing with a lot but still thriving with my team. I was dealing with a lot of real-life issues. Living a life on the road, having to go back and forth to court in New York to handle issues with my son's mother, and trying to make sure my daughter's mom was good often led me to stretches of time at home where I didn't see or communicate with anyone unless it was work-related. It was a lot, but at the same time, I have always been able to realize how fortunate I was to be doing the things God had allowed me. I realized how blessed I was to be able to provide for my kids in a way that some couldn't financially. Once they came into this world, they became my number-one motivation. Every time it seemed like I was faced with an obstacle, there was always another opportunity presented to me that helped me through. Work got better, and opportunities got better as well.

The next big opportunity came at the end of 2010 when "Big Easy" and I were given a second chance to run around the world as contestants on *The Amazing Race*. We were even more excited this time around. We viewed it as a real opportunity to actually win the race this time. The two of us were excited to once again be able to represent ourselves, our families, and our organization on a national network television stage. We were to leave to film the show again for about a month around November to December. This was always good timing for us, as the domestic tour never really kicked off until Christmas. The first time we ran the race, we came in fourth place. We were determined this time around to make that four into a one.

This race was called "Unfinished Business," as all the teams that would be returning were teams who, for the most part, had made simple mistakes that eventually got us all eliminated in the initial season on which we appeared. No teams that had previously ever won the race would be running. So, it was a chance to right the wrong that may have cost us the shot at winning the one-million-dollar prize.

We were not the only ones excited, as the office executives at our company were also excited that we were given a chance to continue to aid in putting the Globetrotters back on the map. At least those who knew we were about to race again were excited, as it always had to be top secret for confidentiality reasons. For me, it was always fun to keep this secret.

One of the differences in this race compared to the first one is that it would start airing during that upcoming domestic tour, which would be great publicity for us and the Globetrotters during the tour. Viewers would have a chance to watch us on television on Sundays and possibly see the team that day or that same week. The timing would be perfect!

The race was filled with teams I had even become fans of during my time watching the show. The "Cowboys," who had just run the season before us, were among my all-time favorite teams, but I knew from my first race experience that it was important to focus, and at the end of the day, you couldn't be a fan of the team or teams that you could be competing against.

This certainly was the case toward the end of that season of filming when we had to make a strategic move to U-turn those same Cowboys in order to gain an advantage. In the end, it was a move we didn't necessarily want to make but had to, as we were the two teams on that particular leg of the race that were in last place out of five teams that remained.

I remember the week that followed that episode after it aired. It was one of the worst weeks of my race experience. Some of the emails we received from fans of the Cowboys were unbelievable to us. I was surprised by how emotionally involved people could become in a reality television show. There were so many racist comments that I stopped reading the emails and eventually deleted my Twitter account. I have since then returned to the Twitter world, but at that time, I was not mentally prepared for that type of backlash simply for trying to win a competition. During that season, "Big Easy" and I did eventually make it to the final three teams.

On the final leg of that season, we traveled from Brazil up to Florida, where the team that finished first on that leg would win the big prize. I would be lying if I told you I wasn't nervous. There were so many things going through my mind, and I bet my partner didn't even know I was having these thoughts. There were things in my head that I should not have had to be thinking during that leg of the race or at all. We wanted to win so bad, but I began to think a lot during the flight from Rio de Janeiro to Miami. I started to think of some of the possible issues I might have to deal with if I won the race—were they even worth it? If I won, how much money would I be expected to keep or give away? Would I be summoned to court with the idea that money was owed to people who had taken no part of what I potentially would win? It was crazy that I was thinking like this, but it was reality. I was almost scared to win. In the end, I didn't have to worry about any of this, as we came in second place.

We had a great time running that final leg but came up just a bit short, eventually having to recognize two very deserving ladies as the winners. We were disappointed not to win, but we knew we had not disappointed anyone who would watch that season. As we had done the season before, we ran the race with class and honor, all the while having fun—the Globetrotter way.

I remember in one of the interviews during the race explaining how excited and blessed I felt to be racing, but how I also encouraged people to be sure to come see us in our element on the court because we were only two of the Globetrotters. We had thirty other players who were just as fun and as likeable as the two of us, and this was a true statement. We had a group of amazing people entertaining fans all around the world. I was so happy to be representing all the guys I had learned from over the years who didn't get the same opportunities I got. I wanted to make those guys proud because I knew many of my former teammates still wanted to be a part of the brand and legacy they helped carry on. It is and was a responsibility to make sure you are not the one to mess up all of that tradition, and it was an honor to represent with that exact mentality.

After running this season of the race, "Big Easy" and I were invited to the main offices in Phoenix for a little recognition gathering with the office employees. For me, it was a big deal, because believe it or not, after about ten years as a player, I still had not been inside our Phoenix headquarters.

Recognition and representing would be no less important that following April, as I, along with several other teammates, would be given the honor of visiting the White House. Just about a week after the race aired in April, I was given the chance to attend the Easter Egg Roll at the White House in our nation's capital. This was an event that I previously had no knowledge of. I had no idea what was in store, and sometimes that was the excitement of being a part of the team—surprises and most of them good surprises. The Easter Egg Roll is an event that takes place annually on the lawn of the White House in Washington, DC. I found out that people across the nation try for years just to get tickets to attend the event, and I would be attending as a Globetrotter with expectations of giving short basketball clinics on the president's court to the kids who would be in attendance. I was just excited to be going to the White House. The only time I had even imagined going to the White House was if I made the NBA and won a championship, but I didn't have to win a championship to get my chance to visit the White House.

We arrived in Washington, DC, the day before the event and got a briefing that night on exactly what we would be doing while there. For the most part, it was business as usual until we found out that the president always stopped by the basketball courts at some point during the event. At this point, it hit me that I might actually meet the president of the United States. I had the privilege of shaking the hand of Governor Bill Clinton before he became president, but I had never met a sitting president. That night, I became so excited that I began to call everyone I knew. It became my mission to be sure to get a photo with the president.

The next day rolled around, and it seemed like we were there for hours on end with no sign of the president. There were several professional athletes on the president's court working with kids attending the event. Half of the court was set up for basketball, and the other half was set up for tennis. Andy Roddick and Chris Evert were the two tennis stars I remember most from the event. I remember Andy because at that time he was probably the best American male tennis player touring, and I remember the fun game of beginner's tennis Chris Evert and I played with the nonofficial rubber tennis ball on the president's court. Let's just say I gave her a little run for her money, and she swore I had played tennis at some point in my life. I honestly didn't recognize who she was at that time. I had heard of her but didn't recognize her for all the accolades she had accomplished over her historic playing career. I told her I never played tennis and that I was just doing what I had seen people on television do. We had a good laugh after our little back and forth, ending with her giving me her tennis cap and telling me I was one of her favorites. My teammate Chris Franklin got a kick out of it, joking with me and saying, "We can't take you nowhere." He referenced this, as just a couple of years earlier, we had attended a celebrity fundraiser poker event in Arizona. At the event, I somehow ended up winning the event. Again, I was just doing what I had seen on television.

Nonetheless, we were finally alerted that the president was about to make his way to the courts. This was evident, as the secret service began to make their way to certain spots on the court. Everyone was excited to shake the hand of the president and, of course, get that photo of the actual act of shaking his hand. President Obama walked onto the court, and everyone stopped what they were doing. Tennis players stopped serving, and us basketball players stopped shooting for a chance to say hello to the president. I would eventually shake hands with the president. I remember trying to hold his hand for an extra second to make sure someone snapped that photo in hopes I would get the photo for a keepsake. That didn't happen. Somehow, my handshake was blocked, but it was okay. I had still met the president. Here I was, a little poor boy from Brinkley, Arkansas, standing on the same court with the president of the United States. I had nothing to be upset about. I was blessed with the sequence of events transpiring in my life.

That same year, I received a really cool email. The email was totally unexpected and came from my college, Centenary College, which I always represented with pride, which was obvious while I raced around the world wearing t-shirts representing the school on national television. Centenary contacted me to inform me I had been elected to go into the Centenary College Athletic Hall of Fame. This brought tears to my eyes. I was thrilled that my school found me worthy of such an honor. The hall of fame was something I never really imagined, and even if it was just my college recognizing me, I knew it was a true blessing. Blessings for me were coming in twos. Two kids, two times on *The Amazing Race*, and that next year, I would get my second chance to meet President Obama.

I think my good friend and colleague Brett Meister, who was head of public relations, must have felt bad about me not getting a good photo the previous year, so he made sure the following year I would have an opportunity to go back. The following year had some of the same celebrities in attendance.

116

Chris Evert and I didn't rematch on the tennis court, but it was cool to meet her for a second time. It was even better to meet the president again. This time around, he spent even more time on the basketball court. I was able to give him some passes as he took jump shots. The rule was if you missed, you had to do push-ups. I stood over the president as he did several push-ups before eventually making a shot off an assisted pass from me.

I was fortunate this time to get photos, including the money shot of shaking President Obama's hand on camera. The president of Brinkley High School class of 1994 was officially documented in a photo with the president. *How lucky can one guy get?* I often asked myself.

If I had a bucket list, I would have just about checked everything off, although there were still several things in life I hoped to experience. One was to go on tour with my team to Australia. This tour was a Globetrotter favorite, according to Globetrotter legends like "Curly" Neal and "Sweet" Lou Dunbar. It was a world away from the world we lived in here in the States. I had been to Australia while running the second season of *The Amazing Race*, but it went by so quickly that I barely remembered being there. Our longtime vice president, Jeff Munn, knew I had never toured there. We talked about it often, and eventually, he made it happen for me, as they had put together a tour not only going to Australia, but also stopping in New Zealand along the way. New Zealand was exciting for me, as my former college teammate Lincoln Abrams had gone to New Zealand shortly after college to pursue his dreams of playing professional basketball. He had made a name for himself in Kiwi land as a really good basketball player, and he had

117

also started a family, which I was very excited to meet. Neither place would disappoint me and my expectations.

I would have a chance on this tour to not only experience down-under Australia life but also a chance to catch up with my former college roommate, who I had started the journey with over fifteen years before as college kids. It was an honor to pay a visit to the school where he doubled up as a math teacher when he was not playing pro ball. Locals called him "The Legend," which was funny to me, but if they viewed him as a legend, it was totally fine in my eyes! These are the type of experiences I never imagined and would not have been forwarded if I had not been living out my dream life.

Australia was great as well. It had been several years since we had played there, so there was certainly a buzz, and most of the games would be performed in front of sold-out crowds. I found both New Zealand and Australia to be so easygoing and laid-back compared to other parts of the world in which I had traveled and performed.

Over a stretch of about four years, I was riding a roller coaster of a life. This roller coaster was more exciting than any coaster I had taken at any amusement park. There was plenty to talk about but nothing to selfishly complain about, as I always kept in my mind and understood that I was doing better than most. Most could not have adjusted to change the way I was able to. This was a great attribute for me, especially with change on the way again, as we were soon to embark upon another transition of ownership of the company. I was also about to embark upon another life-changing moment on my imaginary bucket list.

CHAPTER THIRTEEN

Popes

Toward the end of the 2013 domestic tour, it was pretty well documented that the team was up for sale once again. There was not a shortage of suitors that relished the opportunity to purchase the iconic brand. Shamrock Capital had decided they were ready to let go of ownership, as they had kept control of us for longer than they had originally planned. The one thing they wanted to do was make sure that upon selling the team, it would land in the right hands. They wanted to make sure the brand landed in the hands of people who were interested in continuing to build the brand and who shared some of the same values the Globetrotters had stood for, for over a span of almost ninety years. I would say the people of Shamrock were great owners. They were certainly great for me, but there was a sense of excitement among us players with the idea of who would buy the team next. I remember a meeting towards the end of the tour that year in which the coaches and some of the staff spoke enthusiastically in regard to the coming change and how it would be beneficial to everyone. I certainly bought into the idea, as it had been good to me before; therefore, I had no doubt it would be good again as I headed into my fourteenth season with the organization.

Training camp kicked off that year in late September in Long Island, New York, as it had for several years to that point. Most of us didn't have a real idea of what was happening as far as change in ownership. We were, for the most part, just happy to still have jobs doing what we all loved, and that was putting smiles on the faces of people from all walks of life through the game we loved. A few days into camp, the news was in as to who had purchased the team. We were to keep it a secret for a short while until the deal was finalized. We were to be purchased by Herschend Family Entertainment.

I had never heard of this company, and I had no idea what they were about. When I got the news, my mind immediately went into wonderland, wanting to find out as much about this company as I possibly could. Within the hour of getting the news, I pulled out my phone and started to google. I was impressed with what I read about this company and its historic foundation. There were several things that stood out immediately—one of the first things was family. They are a family-owned company founded in Branson, Missouri. They were built on the foundation of Christian family values. I liked this idea as well. I didn't know a lot of bad Christian people. After further researching, I found out they were the nation's largest family-owned themed attractions corporation; therefore, they were in the business along the lines of what I had been doing throughout my career with the Globetrotters—the business of delivering smiles and entertaining. It was the perfect fit.

Just a few days later, we had a chance to meet the executives and the president of the company, as they came to training camp to fill us in on what was in store for the Globetrotters and tell us firsthand about Herschend Family Entertainment

Company, which at that time was led by Joel Manby. There was a special buzz and heightened curious level of excitement as Joel begin his introduction of Herschend to all of us new family members. He talked about the mission of the company, which was to create memories worth repeating. This was similar to the Globetrotters' mission way before I had even joined the team. This was a mission I had witnessed over my career; I would see the same fans come back each and every year, as it had become tradition for many.

Joel talked about the values of this new company that would now be leading us into forever, as they had no plans of ever selling the team. Values such as exceeding guests' expectations or, in our case, fans' expectations. It was always important for me to surprise fans with how kind I could be. Many times, fans would see us athletes as jerks, but it was always important for me to surprise our Globetrotter fans with how kind and down-to-earth I could be. Other values included serving others, similar to the way we served others in showing up to bring joy to families after natural disasters, the way we showed up at hospitals regularly to visit kids in hospitals, the way we often partnered with organizations like Make-A-Wish to help kids live out their dreams. This partnership was seamless.

Joel spoke about the importance of constantly improving as well as creating emotional connections with our fans. Each and every night as players, we got feedback from fans about how they came to see the Globetrotters as kids and were now bringing their kids to share some of those childhood memories. Often, the parents would say we were as good or even better than they remembered. This was the idea of constantly improving and the creation of emotional connections that made people feel the need to repeat the experience—because the memories put them in such a positive frame of mind. We, as players, could not be more excited.

One of the other things we had found about was that he had appeared on the hit TV show *Undercover Boss*. We were able to see some of the highlights from his appearance during his presentation at training camp that first night. I immediately thought that we had something in common—we had both appeared on popular reality shows.

I was also excited to read Joel's book, *Love Works*. After the meeting that night, I went back to my hotel and purchased Joel's book online. I had not read a book in years, but it was important for me to learn as much as I could about my new bosses. Knowledge of the company along with the ability to listen and learn were a part of what had kept me around for so long. Just from researching the book, I knew the premise was about leading with love.

I'd been lucky to be a part of great change with Shamrock, but I knew if these were the true values of Herschend, then I was ready to once again go all in with my job and my new company.

During one of the practices, Joel and the others had attended Mr. Manby approached a couple of us veteran players during lunch. He spoke with us briefly about some of his ideas for the Globetrotters. He told "Big Easy" and me that he had great respect and appreciation for the way we had represented the brand on such a huge stage like *The Amazing Race*. He told us he wanted us to be a part of the new family and around for as long as we wanted to be around. I was never one to need a pat on the back, but this made me feel really good. Little did he know that "Big Easy" and I were in preparation to run *The Amazing Race* for the third time! It was more reason for us to win this time around while at the same time impressing our new owners.

"Big Easy" and I couldn't believe it. We thought our racing days were over. How many chances would we get? I remember getting the voicemail while on tour in South America that year. Just like the second time, the two of us were not touring together, but at this point in life, communication around the world was as easy as knocking on a neighbor's door.

"Did you get the call?" That would be the question.

"Yep!" How could or would we say no? No way we would, and just as we had two years before, we would be racing around the world around November to December. This was to be another season aired during the domestic tour. We were excited to run the race, and we were excited to kick of the tour that year under new ownership.

As usual, things were going well for me. It was a really exciting time. We could all feel the level of change and excitement. We all begin to feel more important, and we also felt under Herschend that our feelings and opinions mattered. We were all being treated better than ever. During the domestic tour early in 2014, I was given a new and special assignment. I was informed via email from our vice president, Jeff, that I would be taking a group of our guys on a short two-week tour of France as a player-coach. This tour was to happen about a month into the domestic tour. I was beyond tickled for the opportunity. Jeff had always been one who believed in me, as far back as I could remember. It was a chance for me to expand and possibly extend my career, as we all know athletes can't play forever.

As player-coach, I would be in charge of an entire tour entourage of about twenty-four personnel. Many people who attend a Globetrotter event may see a coach and not realize how important they are to the operation, but their responsibilities go far beyond the court. It's a great responsibility that not many are given during their stints with the team. I knew I had it in me, and I was excited for the challenge. I was always a fan of traveling abroad anyway; I realized how lucky I was to be able to make a living doing something many people saved and spent their life savings to do. The tour was a success, as Kurt and Jeff would tell me on their visit to France during the tour.

I had always observed and known what to do. I was so thankful that I'd been blessed with the ability to lead in a way that people would want to work and do well for me as a leader. It was leading with love. I was able to apply this mentality to my first tour as a coach. After that tour ended, we all made our ways back to our respective teams, as we had three domestic tours going on simultaneously during the early parts of the year. The tour was really good for me mentally as well. I was now for sure recognized as a leader and a person who could be relied on by the company. Realizing you can't do all the things you were able to do when you first started your career as a player can be a tough pill to swallow, but I never had a problem with new talent and seeing my colleagues get opportunities. It was important for me to be the veteran player who had no problem giving younger players the same opportunities and shine I was able to experience.

This was something that was not super common in my line of work. Some of the guys I came up playing with fought tooth and nail to hang on to every moment of show-shine they could retain. Even before the coaching opportunity, I was secure in me and what was in store for me; therefore, I was more apt to help and encourage as opposed to making things difficult for the new generation of talent coming along to possibly replace me. I knew that we were all replaceable, and I also knew that in order to have a long career, you needed to be able to change and adapt to new generations and new ways.

Speaking of change, not much changed with "Big Easy" and me as far as our luck on *The Amazing Race* was concerned. For the third time, we would come up short. In that particular season, we finished sixth among the race contestants. That was our worst finish of the three. It was okay, though, because once again, we had represented the brand the Globetrotter way—having fun while trotting the globe. I remember watching that final episode in Canada. I was there to promote games for the tour that would be headed to Canada just a couple weeks after the airing of the race had completed. *The Amazing Race* is a really popular show up there, and I became a constant in the media there over the years to help promote and try to boost ticket sales in Canada. I didn't mind at all. The little fame I experienced there was pretty cool. It was just enough. It was funny to me that when I was in street clothes in Canada, I was recognized more than I was in the States. Kurt's vision had really taken off in Canada! The combination of Kurt's vision and the new ownership had everyone feeling good about what we were building.

The summer that followed the domestic tour that year was pretty quiet for me. My best friend on the team, "Big Easy," got married, which was the highlight of the summer for me. Many of the younger guys were doing awesome events at Silver Dollar City theme park in Branson, Missouri, where our new Herschend Family of owners had originated. Guys seemed to love being there, and they bragged on how kind the actual family members were in treating them while working those live events.

Live events were just the tip of the iceberg of ideas they had in store for the Globetrotter side of the company. Training camp would come around again with many players returning. One of the visions Kurt had was not to have as much turnover of players year to year. He wanted to create stars that fans would want to come back and see every year. Developing relationships, so to speak. Herschend seemed to be on the same page as Shamrock had been with regard to this. There seemed to be a bit more commitment and security for us as players, which, in turn, made it easier for us to perform each and every night. The domestic tour of 2015 was set to be more exciting than any other, as we could all see the commitment Herschend was putting into the organization. Everything was getting better!

We were getting better things like better uniforms, more equipment, as well as more days off on the tour, which was something we all supremely appreciated, as in the past, sometimes we would perform thirty consecutive days with no days off.

For me, the domestic tour that year was pretty short. I had been selected to go on the two-month European tour that would travel to about ten countries. This was the first time I had been on this extended tour in a few years, and I was excited, as Europe was my first international tour as a Globetrotter.

My mind was in a good and different place this time around. I had my mind made up that I would try to take more advantage of the opportunity to see more of the beautiful places we would be traveling. In all the years before, I'd never been a good tourist when it came to my travels. I would spend my daytime sleeping until it was time to leave for the show and my nighttime partying when I could. I made a promise to myself that I would get out during the days and sightsee. For a couple of guys on the tour, it was their first time in Europe. As soon as we touched down in Europe, they were counting down the days until we were to go home, which was almost two months. I explained to them how ridiculous it was to do this, also letting them know how fortunate they were to be traveling the world. They took my advice and eventually ended up having the time of their lives. I think they continued to count down, but they didn't let me know about it until we were down to about five days of tour left.

It was refreshing, as no matter the city we were in, each day, I would get to the hotel, drop my bags, and take a walk. I would walk to the center of the city and take in any sights or culture I could indulge in with the free time I had. Some days, it would be two or three hours, but I was sure to get out regardless. I began to post on my Instagram, sharing with those fans of mine who lived vicariously through my travels.

Ironically, on this same tour, I got what I now consider the coolest opportunity of my life. A couple of weeks before the European tour ended, I got an email from our main offices that several of us players had been chosen to travel to Rome and meet Pope Francis. Pope Francis had quickly gained legendary status as the pope and was often referred to as the people's pope—even I knew this. This was for sure a once-in-a-lifetime opportunity, as I had once missed the opportunity to meet the pope. I knew all about the pope and the honor it was to have a chance to meet him. In November of 2000, at the start of my second season with the Globetrotters, several of my teammates traveled to Rome to meet Pope John Paul II.

I recall how big of a deal this event was. It was all over the media, as we had made Pope John Paul II an honorary Globetrotter during the visit. I was now on the back end of my playing career, and this event had come around again for me. I immediately called my father, who is a youth minister, to brag about what I was to be doing in the coming days. He was immediately jealous, asking me, "How does one get to meet the pope?" I jokingly told him all you had to do was hit him up on social media. This, of course, was not true, but it was happening. There were two of my teammates who would be traveling from home to Rome to meet the pope, joining my teammate "Ant" Atkins and me along with our CEO, Kurt Schneider, and our head of public relations, Brett Meister, who was actually the person who had made this happen.

For "Ant" and me, it was perfect since we did not have to travel very far at all, as our tour was in Italy at that time. All we had to do was jump on a train to Rome and we would be there. Once we arrived in Rome, the hype and excitement become more prevalent. Shortly after arriving in Rome, we were to meet with Brett, Kurt, and our other teammates "Big Easy" and "Hi-Lite" Bruton. During the meeting that night at the hotel, we talked about what we hoped to happen and if certain things happened how we would approach the pope. Turns out we had traveled to Rome, but there was no guarantee that we would actually meet the pope. We would have front row seats up close and personal for the weekly mass—a mass which thousands of tourist and onlookers travel from all corners of the world to attend just to get a glimpse of the pope.

The morning came, and it was time to make our way to Vatican City. Before my visit to the Vatican, I was unaware that it was considered its own country and is the smallest country in the world. You can find out lots of fun facts about this place on Google. We arrived at the Vatican just as the thousands of fans who had come to see the pope arrived as well. I had no idea of the magnitude of the situation in these moments. It was much bigger than I had imagined or anticipated. We made our way through the tightly secured gates. We had seats just beneath the lowest stairs that led up to where the pope would be delivering mass. The morning was really hot! I was sweating like I had never sweat before. It was partly due to the heat, but it was also due to the pressure Kurt was putting on me in regards to being responsible for spinning the ball on the finger of the pope if the opportunity were to present itself.

Before we knew it, the pope had arrived. We knew he had made his entrance, as the crowd begin to roar as the pope mobile maneuvered its way through the parted lanes in the square of Vatican City. Cameras were out and flashing as the pope made his way through the audience, stopping to shake hands with a few of the worshipers and onlookers. Handshakes they would never forget. Pope Francis eventually made his way to his regular position in the square, where he delivered his weekly message. He delivered his message as he always did; as it came to a close, we were informed that we would, indeed, have the opportunity to meet him. We were told that he always made his way down toward where the sick kids were seated when he was finished mass. We were to make our way over there at the same time. At this point, there was no towel or fan that could dry me from the sweat and nerves that had overcome my mind and body.

We waited as Pope Francis made his way down toward us. I stood on the far end, holding the basketball as Pope Francis began to shake hands with my teammates and owner. He joked with "Ant," saying, "You small." As he made his way toward me, I could hear him say as he shook each one our hands, "Pray for me." I later found out he says that to just about everyone. I shook his hand last, and he made his way to the center of us for a photo opportunity, where we presented him with a framed jersey, making Pope Francis an honorary Globetrotter. All I could hear in my ear was our CEO saying, "Spin the ball on his finger, Herb. Spin the ball on his finger!" Hell, I was so nervous I couldn't spin the ball on my own finger. I eventually got the pope to hold his finger up. I feared the ball might spin off and hit the pope in the head. I would forever be the guy who hit the pope in the face with a basketball if this happened. I eventually put the ball on his finger for a split second. It was one of my worst spins ever, but it was just long enough to call it a spin. This spin ended up being one of the biggest media impressions in our organization's history.

130

We had become the story that day and the several days that followed. That was the power of the Globetrotters. That visit to Vatican City became the day Pope Francis played basketball with the Globetrotters. I was a part of history. I am forever grateful for that opportunity, as I had not ever been so nervous in my Globetrotter career. I was not even nervous when I met President Obama twice, but the one time I met the pope, something came over me. Kurt, Brett, and the rest of my teammates had some good laughs about the visit. In the end, it was a successful trip and worth every drop of sweat I dripped on the pope's hand that afternoon! The summer of tours that followed this European tour and the visit with the pope turned into what I consider my best summer ever.

Within a week of getting home from Europe, I was set to go back to New Zealand and Australia with some of my other team members. We were to finish that same tour off in South Africa. South Africa is a country I visited on my own one summer, as I had begun to take at least one personal international trip after every yearly tour. I was excited to go there with my teammates for the first time. The New Zealand and Australia tour would go off great as usual. The bad thing was that the South Africa part of the tour was cancelled, sending us home several days early. I was disappointed not to be traveling to South Africa with my teammates, but as soon as I found out about the tour being cancelled, I emailed the main offices about possibly going on the South America tour that was happening within a few days of me getting home. I had grown to love the South American tour. They granted my request.

I was given another chance to go as player-coach. I was thrilled, and the players who were on the tour were thrilled to have me. During my career, I was never one to shy away from the work or the travel. Over the years, some guys would dread tours and didn't want to even go sometimes. I was the exact opposite. I got excited to go home only the day before it was time. I found it important to live in the moment, as I knew there were so many of my former teammates who wished they had a chance to do some things all over again. As a player-coach, one thing I loved was being able to tell guys how to improve as well as being able to go on the court during a game and show them exactly what I meant. It was leading with love and leading by example. It was being consistent each and every day. I feel that as a leader of men, it's important to be consistent. Consistency allows players to know that each and every day, they will get the same leader. No matter what you deal with as a leader, it is important to not let your body language display your actual mood. Those who follow detect this, and when it happens regularly, it gives them a sense of "here we go today—our leader is having a bad day." I have stated many times here that all of my days were not good, but I knew how to deal.

I had one of my worst days after that training camp of 2015. Camp went great as usual. After camp, most of the guys headed home to prepare for whatever tours they were assigned to. I was selected to stay for a couple of days for an appearance on *Good Morning America*. On this appearance, we were to announce the start of the upcoming tour and to also proclaim courageous cancer-surviving host Robin Roberts an honorary Globetrotter. The day was fun, and it was a breeze. But I was not prepared for what was in store for me when I got home that night.

I got to my apartment that night and decided to check my mail, as I had not been home for a couple weeks. The mail was full, and there was one piece of mail from a New York court that stood out. I opened it, and what I read broke my heart. I was being summoned to court for child support issues. I was totally blindsided. I had never missed any payments, and I had just visited New York the month before with my daughter traveling with me. I guess it was just the way it had to be. With all the good that had happened that year, there had to be something to damper it. It sent me into a two-week depression. It would have a lingering effect on me, but I eventually was able to accept what was happening and prepare to move forward with it.

At least I still had my job. At least I was not living some crazy lifestyle to where I couldn't deal with the possibility of change. At that time, it was just what was meant to be. I was never handed anything I couldn't handle, so I knew I would move forward and continue to take the good with the bad, and for the most part, life was all good. *Mr. Pope, please pray for me*, were my thoughts!

CHAPTER FOURTEEN

Pressure, Success, and Shock

Merriam-Webster defines "pressure" as the burden of physical or mental distress. One of the definitions of "success" is a favorable or desired outcome. You might ask why I have defined these words. Well, the reason is because too much pressure or lack of success can lead you into shock. "Shock" is defined by Merriam-Webster as a sudden or violent mental disturbance: a disturbance in the equilibrium or permanence of something.

The reason I decided to title this chapter the way I did is because in this chapter, I experienced pressure, success, and shock. How you deal with pressure can determine how successful you become. We all put certain levels of pressures on ourselves. In most cases, we pressure ourselves by setting goals, which sometimes determine how we view ourselves. We ask ourselves, *Am I a success*? If we reach these goals, we say yes. If we can't seem to reach these goals, we tend to view ourselves as failures. These failures can send our minds and bodies into shock. Shock can also occur when the success we have attained turns into what one might view as failure, as sometimes sudden changes occur. How we deal with the shock after the failures will determine if we can attain success that we once strived for.

I was not in a good place after I returned home from training camp of 2015. I was lucky I didn't have to sit home long to think about what I was dealing with, as work always had a way of helping me escape reality. What better way to escape than my assignment to be coach on the upcoming military tour.

Instead of *The Amazing Race,* this winter I was assigned to coach the military tour. We were to leave just after Thanksgiving for a two-week tour of USA military bases across Europe and the Middle East. The military tour was always one of the most gratifying, and it was just what I needed at that time. We went to some awesome bases during the course of the tour, allowing us to bring a taste of home to our troops and their families. Being able to bring a taste of home over the holiday season to those sacrificing for us always eased the mind. One of the things about going on the military tour was that at some point during that upcoming domestic tour, I would be eligible for my player legacy leave to go home for a few days.

I had requested my vacation to go home around Mardi Gras in Louisiana. Having lived in Louisiana for over twenty years, I felt it was a good time for me to go and experience the Mardi Gras spectacle for once in my life. It didn't disappoint. I had a blast, as I had now begun to experience things that were right at my fingertips that I hadn't previously taken advantage of. It was a good break from the tour, but I was certainly ready to get back on the road after the short visit home was over.

This tour would be filled with many firsts for me. During this tour, I would be allowed to go to a couple of places and territories I had never been before. The first one was Puerto Rico. We had in past recent years done tours to Puerto Rico during the domestic tour. Finally, I would have my chance to go, as I was again entrusted to lead a group on that particular tour. It was a great tour, and happening moves were being made.

In March of that same tour, the main offices were officially relocated and opened in Atlanta, Georgia. We were no longer based in Phoenix. I felt this was a great move. All of the Herschend businesses were based there, so we may as well all be under one roof. I felt Atlanta was a great location for many reasons such as the same reasons over ninety years before, the team had been named after Harlem back in the early 1900s, as the forefront of African-American entertainment in the States was in Harlem, New York. The team actually originated in Chicago, but it was obviously a good move going with this name. Today, many might say Atlanta is the new Harlem with all of the African-American entertainers and companies that have been established there over recent years. It was a good place to be, and I was a part of it all. Being a part of it put me in a position to brag and boast to some of my former teammates whom I kept in contact with about how great the new owners were. I would tell them often how great things were and how I wished many of them were still around to enjoy some of the fruits of the hard work they had put in over the years. The Globetrotters were exactly where they needed to be under the ownership and leadership of Herschend.

As the 2016 tour went about, I took a group of players on a couple different tours, not just the Puerto Rico tour. I took a group across parts of New England domestically as well as internationally to Mexico. Mexico had, to this point, also become one of my favorite places to tour, as the fans always came to have a great time. As the tour ended, I remember enquiring to our vice president about possibly adding me to the end of the domestic tour, which would be finishing in Hawaii and Alaska.

Like always, he granted my request, allowing me to relieve one of our coaches to go home early for some rest time. The reason I really wanted to go on this tour was to complete my travel of all fifty states. I had been to and performed in every state except Alaska. This tour would allow me to complete the fifty, and it also allowed me to fly my daughter over to Hawaii, as she was not happy with me for going the previous year and not inviting her. I was able to settle two birds with one stone.

As the Alaska tour ended, some of the good changes were becoming more evident. Herschend brought all Globetrotter coaches to a leadership conference to reiterate the mission and values upon which the company was built and to be run. This was something never offered before and something beneficial to all of those in attendance, especially those who had not read the book *Love Works,* which I would again recommend to anyone in a leadership position. Things were moving fast and smooth over the summer.

Shortly after the meetings I would get my next assignment. I was to coach another quick tour taking us down to Uruguay and Bolivia. Many people may not know, but basketball is beloved in Uruguay. It will never take the place of soccer, but every time we traveled there, we played in front of sold-out arenas—just awesome people and fans who made it easy to perform.

Tours made it so much easier for me to take my mind away from reality. A reality that I would face when I returned home.

After the quick South America tour, I made it home, and, like always, I checked my mail. The decision was in the mail—my child support judgment. The decision I received was not favorable for me, but it was not beyond unfair. That day led me to another decision; I decided I would not have any more children. For my fortieth birthday, I decided to end that possibility and treated myself to a trip to the Summer Olympics in Rio de Janeiro, Brazil. People were up in a rage about the possibility of the Zika virus, but not me. One thing I learned in my travels even before the popularity of fake news was not to believe everything you see on American news television. If I lived with this fear, there was no way I could be a Globetrotter. Fear of travel was not an option, and due to the threat of the Zika virus, I had a chance for a trip of a lifetime for a reasonable coast. It was a great decision.

I flew down with one piece of carry-on luggage and a backpack. Over the course of the six-day solo trip, I was able to attend six events, three of which I had never attended before. I had the chance to see Michael Phelps swim as well as watch Usain Bolt mesmerize an entire stadium with his speed and showmanship. After attending these summer Olympic games, I vowed that God willing, I would be attending the 2020 Tokyo, Japan, summer games.

The summer had been good to me, and at forty years old, I was looking forward to what work had in store for me, as training camp this year would finally be at a new location. Training camp was set for December 2016 in Atlanta, Georgia, the new headquarters of the Harlem Globetrotters. We were all excited. It was business as usual, as each and every year we were to see our doctors to complete physical examinations showing we were fit to participate in training camp as well as the upcoming world tour. "Was" is the key word for me this particular year. I went in to my doctor, who I had been going to for years, and for the first time, I didn't pass my physical. He told me my blood pressure was too high for him to pass me, and he immediately sent me to see a specialist. I was freaking out, to say the least.

The new doctor sent me for testing and all kinds of work to try to pinpoint the problem. He immediately put me on meds to try to level out my blood pressure. He told me to return in a week, assuring me he would pass me once the meds started to work and when the test results came back. He told me that many athletes and people in general dealt with this problem of high blood pressure. I found out after some questioning of my mom that it was more than likely a hereditary thing for me. Both my mom's and dad's sides of the family had a history of high blood pressure. I would eventually return to the doctor a week later to find that all of the tests came back good, and he would pass me, therefore making me good to go for training camp. The only thing was that now I was on blood pressure medication. I had never been on medication in my entire life, but things had apparently changed at forty.

I was feeling so much pressure. I was trying to figure what I was going to do if I couldn't play anymore. How would I pay my bills? How would I take care of my kids and maintain the child support I was ordered to pay, which had just recently been raised? I wondered if I would get fired or if my team would find another role for me if I didn't pass the physical. Thank God I did pass—for the time being, I was good to go back to work doing what I loved.

As I headed into year eighteen, training camp was the best ever. Everything about camp was good. The team buses were new. The facilities were state of the art. The schedule was good and beneficial to everyone. The hotel was top of the line. We had always stayed at top-of-the-line places and did things first class for the most part, but now things were business class. We even had a banquet at the end of training camp.

The banquet was a time for all of the people of the Globe-trotter organization to come together for fellowship and rec-ognition of the commitment many had made to the company over time. This was something I never imaged happening and something my past teammates would have died to see. It was a great event! We had a chance to see and meet some of the peo-ple who worked in the offices, and they had a chance to meet and greet with the players who they worked so hard for every day, making sure things went well when we were trotting the globe. The event was great for team building and comradery. The event was such a success that I knew it would be some-thing we would look forward to each and every year for many years to come. It was a great way to start the tour, as we would all go home for a few days after that training camp and prepare to leave for the domestic tour Christmas day, which was just about ten days away.

I knew in my heart this was going to be the best tour of all my previous seventeen. Things were great. As the tour sched-ule and assignments developed, I noticed I would be doing a lot of promoting during the tour. It's what we called advanced work. I was basically a week on tour and a week on the road promoting shows for upcoming cities. The promoting was a good way to get away from the day to day, but I always missed being away from the team.

One of my jobs on tour as assistant coach was to make sure everyone got frequent days off. This was an idea that was never a priority in years past. I made sure I had a schedule where guys knew they would have a day or so to refresh so they could continue to perform at the highest levels during the tour. Even when I was away from the tour, I had to make sure guys were taking their much-needed time off. I never even put myself down for days off. I often felt I would be missing something if I was on tour and not at the arenas. I was away from the team plenty to where I didn't need to be in the off-day rotation, so I carried on accordingly.

Promoting was going well. I was doing promotions in all of the major markets across the United States. Los Angeles; Washington, DC; New York City. You name a major market, and I was there, promoting the shows. I was doing shows like *The Today Show* and *Good Morning America* again, even being sent over to Europe to promote the European tour with my fellow player-coach "Slick" Shaw.

We were excited for the opportunity to go to Europe as player-coaches and a couple of the longest tenured players on the team. We always worked together, and our promotions across Europe wouldn't prove any different, as our vice president praised us for the rise in ticket sales as a result of the work we had done while in Europe. It was good work and good times for the two of us. The work was long, but the work was fun. We enjoyed the time in Europe, but by the end of the advanced work, we were ready to rejoin our teams.

When I returned back stateside, I was only with the team for a day or so before heading off to do more advanced work and promoting upcoming events. I was attending events for organizations like the American Red Cross, which we had recently partnered up with. I had doubled back to New York again for more work, as we were to be the first team to perform in the newly renovated Nassau Coliseum on Long Island. I was busy! I was super busy promoting. Not a lot of coaching or playing was going on at this time, but no complaints here, as I enjoyed every aspect of my job. It was a blessing to be busy, for sure. The mass media tour would end up in Canada, one of my favorite stops, where I would do a week of promoting before heading back to the States to end my tour in the New Nassau Coliseum, where I had previously done some promoting. I didn't perform that day, but it was nice to be able to see the transformation of such an historic arena which I had performed in many times over the course of many years! Like always, I was ready to go home for a little break when it was time.

Within days of returning home from tour, I got a devastating call from my father that one of my closest cousins had passed. It was a total shock to all of us. He was just one year older than I was. How could this happen to such a young and healthy man? I didn't understand but had to deal. How come it seemed when I was doing so well and having so much success I was always blindsided with something to bring me back down to the realities of life? Attending this funeral brought back so many memories for me. The times I would visit them in Memphis on the Greyhound bus with my Grandma Mamie. The times I would be outside taking shots on their hoops during my summer visits. The fishing trips. It really put things in perspective. Much of my motivation and drive had come from the time I had spent with him and his family as a kid. We were all in shock, but at the same time, we knew there was nothing we could do about it. One thing that always helped me was getting away and traveling.

After the funeral, I did some things to take my mind away. I took a road trip down to Houston to take in an Astros baseball game. On that same trip, I drove over to New Orleans to take in some Jazz Fest festivities, an event I had always wanted to attend. I knew I needed to do these things for my sanity; otherwise, I would certainly fall back in a place I hated being, and that was depression. I always did everything I could to stay away from those draining thoughts. The next thing I did was plan a trip to Europe.

I went to Belgium and Holland. These were two places that were always dear to me, as Belgium was the first country I had ever traveled to outside the United States. It was refreshing and much needed. It allowed me to reset my mind. I took in some local things in Holland like bike riding. I rented a bike and rode all around the city as the locals and many visitors do. I knew I had to do things that would keep me busy, as I had to do whatever it took to keep a strong mind. After a good week of relaxing and enjoying Europe, I made my way back home. I was ready to relax and prepare for whatever was next workwise. I returned home that Monday. I would always take a full day to regroup and try to get myself reacquainted with local time following international trips. This is exactly what I did that Tuesday. I slept most of that day, doing much of nothing.

Then Wednesday happened. Wednesday, May 24, 2017, I woke up to an early phone call like the ones I always dreaded. It was my high school girlfriend calling to inform me that her mother, Mrs. Wallace, had passed away. It didn't come as a total surprise, as I knew she had fallen ill and didn't have much time, but it was certainly a time for reflection. I took that time to think about all the things she had taught me about business and success. The stories I mentioned about how she introduced me to the family business of her funeral home. Such a great woman had been taken away from us, but we were all so lucky to have had the time with her, as she has lived over ninety years. After sobbing, I eventually got up to get my day going, deciding to link up with one of my best friends and former college basketball teammates, Aljay Foreman, for a drink and lunch. The events that happened after this led me to where I am now writing this book.

Aljay and I had just sat down and made an order when my phone rang. It was my teammate "Slick." I took the call. "Slick" was calling to let me know that he had just received a phone call informing him that he would no longer be a part of the Globetrotters. He had called to thank me for all the good times we shared together on the road. I was immediately saddened and sickened to hear the news, as I knew how hard he worked and how far he had come as a member of the organization. What could I say? It was business as usual. I told "Slick" that if he ever needed anything to feel free to call me, as we were brothers for life. After uttering these words to "Slick," I said to him jokingly, "Man, I better check my phone to see if I may have missed that same call of being let go." He laughed that I had nothing to worry about. As he liked to say, I was ice water. I didn't really think my job was in jeopardy since I had always only ever been told to keep up the good work.

We eventually hung up the phone, and I stepped outside to check my voicemail, as I had a message from our offices. It was a call telling me to call back at my earliest convenience. I immediately called back and was sent to voicemail. Within five minutes, I got a phone call—the same unexpected phone call I had just joked with "Slick" about possibly getting. The call was to tell me that after eighteen years of service, my services were no longer needed. I can't put into words the feeling I had hearing these words. I was immediately spaced out. I didn't feel sad. I was too shocked to feel sad. I went back into the restaurant to tell my best friend of the news. I sat there for five minutes before leaving him a twenty-dollar bill on the table, as I began to feel sick and needed to go home. The feelings I felt for the next twenty-four hours would be impossible to put into words. The best way to describe it is to imagine the worst thing to ever happen to you in your life happening. That's the feeling. It was totally unexpected shock to say the least.

What a day that was for me. I had to deal with death and losing my career on the same day. I choose not to go into any detail past this day in regard to my job, but I will end by saying it got me here, to where I am currently, one year later writing the final chapter of this book and feeling super motivated. Never burn a bridge, and always stay motivated!

★

Closing

In closing, there are a few more things I would like to talk about in regard to me and the beautiful life I have been blessed to live up to this point. I have always been a positive and motivated person. That will never change. In my life, I have had many ups and downs. For the most part, I have endured many more ups than downs. I am very lucky and often referred to by my mom as the chosen one. We all know how a mom generally loves her children. There is nothing like that feeling from a parent. As I mentioned here in the book, I always tell my son no matter what he does in life not to ever disappoint his mom, nor should he ever make her cry unless the tears are tears of joy.

In life, I have always been self-motivated. Self-motivation comes from within. Some of us have to dig deeper than others to discover these levels of motivation within us. I have never needed anyone to make me do things in life, especially when it came to things such as learning, helping others, and training myself. These are things I did and do for me because I want to do everything in my control to reach my full potential, and I will continue to do these things throughout life.

At the same time, I am a true believer that every person was not born with the same opportunities and cognitive abilities. It's important that we sometimes take a step back and mentally put ourselves in the positions of others. Close our eyes for minutes at a time to get a sense of what another person's life and mindset could be. This is something I have always been able to do and even more so in the year after retiring from basketball and doing things like ride-share driving. It's been refreshing for me. We also need to understand that just because people don't do exactly what we want or expect them to do doesn't make them bad people. In life, we can't always have everything our way.

I have learned throughout life that as long as you do what people want or expect you to do, you become the best person in the world in that person's eyes. When you don't succumb to certain requests, the opposite opinion is easily formed. That's just human nature. It doesn't make us bad people. Sometimes we, as individuals, can be very selfish, but that's not always a bad thing either. At the end of the day, you have to look out for what's best for you and your family, if that's one of the many things that drive you.

In my life, I have always dreamed big and set lofty expectations for the things I have and will achieve. During my journey, I have had to deal with disappointment, but at the same time, lots of joy and happiness. It's all a part of life. As a young boy, I dreamed big, and most of my dreams have come true as a result of the way I have treated people along the way.

In the book, you see how there was always someone putting their reputation on the line forwarding me opportunities. These people knew me for the person I was, and they knew my levels of commitment to things when given a chance. I'm happy to know that every time anyone has taken a chance on me, I have excelled, in most cases exceeding expectations.

During some of the dark moments I've had after my eighteen-year career traveling the world with my team, I have always been able to find light in the dark. I have even gone to counseling, something I never had the courage to do before. There is nothing wrong with seeking council in hopes of bettering oneself.

Since stepping away from the game, I have started doing things like running more. I have skied for the first time in my life. I have taken a liking to outdoors activities like hiking. I attended Super Bowl week and NBA all-star weekend for fun and networking.

Writing this book has been therapeutic for me. Over the years of sharing stories with friends and family, it was often said that I should write a book. It took me being away from the one thing I was committed to for the longest part of my life to find the courage to share my story. Writing this book was quite the experience. It took me down memory lane. Things I had not thought about in years came back to me during this process. I shed many tears while writing, but I had abundantly more smiles and literal out-loud laughing while writing this book.

In this world we live in nowadays, many people write books about their lives. What's different about my book? Nothing. The difference is, it's my story and I didn't have to do any research to write it. I only had to relive my life.

When my eighteen-year career came to an end, many people were in shock, including myself. It took me months to make it public that I was done. I am secure in knowing I did everything in my career the best way I could and in the right way. In my departure, I was given exactly these sentiments from the organization that gave me this nearly twenty-year career. Life can be full of regret. No one I know has ever lived a life with no regrets. We have to learn to build and become better people in that we have minimal regret moving forward. Therefore, we have to live our best life. Always be cognizant of the way you treat people because you never know when you will need that same person. Never burn a bridge, because when you do things the wrong way and burn bridges, oftentimes it's impossible to go back. Be good for goodness's sake, with no expectations or rewards as a result. Also, there is nothing wrong with having more than one dream. I dreamed, lived a dream, and now I'm dreaming again. Dreams do come true. I am an example. Live in the moment, and take full advantage of the moments while within them. Opportunities come often— you just have to recognize them. I am thrilled and excited to share my story with the world. I learned so much during my travels.

Fans of mine and people close to me who followed my career assumed that when I was done, I should easily be able to get job on television with all the television experiences I'd had. It's not that easy, nor would I want it to be. It's a new grind filled with excitement and unlimited potential. The year following my career has been filled with so much creation. Brinkley High School gave me a diploma. Four years at Centenary College earned me a bachelor's degree—a degree in education that made me eligible to educate. I often said I was lucky to not be limited to teaching in one school because as a Globetrotter,

I was able to educate all over the world. Eighteen years with the Harlem Globetrotters gave me a PhD in entertainment, ideas, creativity, and philanthropy. Ideas including game shows, motivational speaking, and television shows, just to name a few ideas in my mind now. These things will happen because I'm claiming them and I'm not one to just sit on my hands waiting for these ideas to magically happen. I am working on these ideas every day. I am so thankful for everyone who has supported me and continues to support me.

There are some people I personally want to thank. Obviously, I would like to thank my parents, grandparents, aunts, uncles, and siblings. I want to thank all of my teachers, especially my high school basketball coach, Herbert Williams, for making me the man I am today. Thanks to all of my friends and family. Thanks to all of my teammates and the touring staff who worked with me along the way. Special thanks to Steve Feit for always supporting me. Thanks to the mothers of my children for giving me two awesome kids and raising them the right way. I would like to thank all the schools I attended: Partee Elementary, Brinkley High School, and Centenary College. Many thanks to all of the people who employed me with jobs and opportunities: Walmart, Harvey's Fish Farm, Branscumb Funeral Home, Fitness World, and Harlem Globetrotters International as well as colleagues who up to this point gave me the best ride of my life. Big thanks to CBS and *The Amazing Race* for the chance to show the world who I am on a national television stage. Special thanks to the creators of that show, Bertram and Elise. Thanks to all the people I have lived with over the years. You all have positively influenced me in my life.

Thank you for taking time out to learn more about me. Last but not least, I want to thank God for creating me and watching over me at all times. Anyone wanting to contact me for advice, events, or anything, all you have to do is reach out. I'm not that hard to find! Be blessed, encouraged, and stay motivated!

★
Photo Gallery

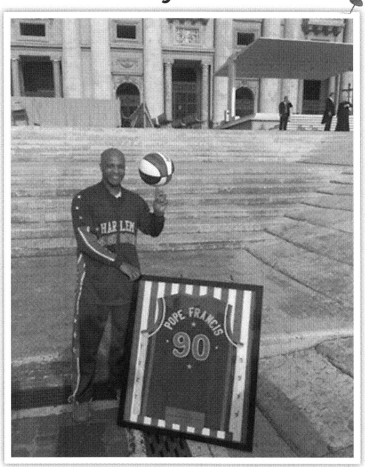

At the Vatican

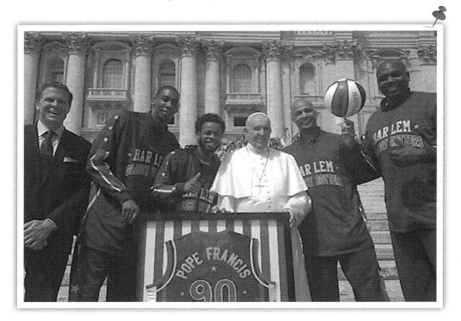

With the Pope

Coaching President Obama

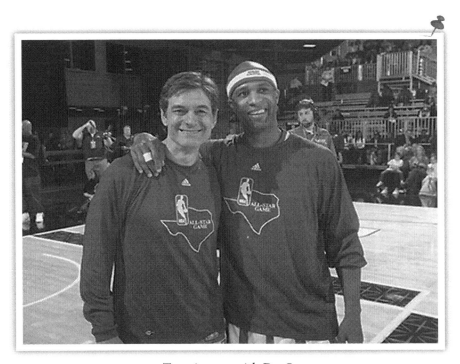

Teaming up with Dr. Oz

Getting advice from Warren Buffet

Competing on The Amazing Race with If Big Easy

A really Amazing Race

On The Price Is Right

Making a school visit

Having fun back at school

Encouraging the troops in Afghanistan

Supporting the Red Cross

School Visit

Coach Herbert Williams

Son Nicholas

Daughter Reya

162

2- Year Old Herbert

Dad Herbert

Big Easy and Herbert

My favorite teacher, Ms. Louise Mitchell

Sister Iesha, Mom Linda, Herbert, Sister Shammik and Sister Aireal

Mom (Linda) and Herbert

Herbert, Reya and Nicholas

★
About The Author

Originally from Brinkley, Arkansas. In Brinkley Herbert Lang was an All-State Standout athlete also graduating at the top of his class while serving as senior class president. Herb went on to college graduating with a bachelor's degree in health and physical education from Centenary College of Louisiana in Shreveport. He played for the Harlem Globetrotters for 18 years. Throughout his travels some of his most memorable moments include meeting Pope Francis, President Obama, and appearing on numerous nationwide television commercials and reality TV shows, most notably on CBS's *The Amazing Race* for three seasons. He currently resides in Sacramento, California. He is a proud father of two Nicholas and Reya Lang.

Post Globetrotting Herb has ventured into many different avenues building on the wealth of knowledge accumulated through life and his travels to nearly 90 countries worldwide.

Herb is an active speaker, coach, and motivator while also having his hand in entertainment. He is currently working with a major Hollywood TV production company in further developing one of his many TV show concepts. Herb is a true believer in his idea that we as individuals should treat others even better than we expect to be treated! He feel success is not determined by how much money we make, but how many lives we touch along the way! He is inspired in knowing that the journey depicted in his book will motivate and inspire people from all ages and backgrounds.

★

Character Index

Meister, Brett,

Munn, Jeff,

Neal, Fred "Curly,"

Obama, Barack,

Paul II, Pope John,

Payton, Walter,

Phelps, Michael,

Richardson, Nolan,

Richardson, Chris "Flash,"

Roberts, Robin,

Roddick, Andy,

Sandler, Adam,

Schneider, Kurt,

Shaw, Willie "Slick,"

Sihatrai, Allen,

Sinclair, Clyde "The Glide,"

Strawberry, Darryl,

Swanigan, Ellious "Snowman,"

Wallace, Barbara,

Wallace, Sherra "Pooh,"

Williams, Herbert (Coach),

Williams, Marlon,

Williamson, Corliss,

🌐 www.herblang.com

f www.facebook.com/herbertflighttime.lang

📷 www.instagram.com/datrotter4

🐦 twitter.com/datrotter4

in www.linkedin.com/in/herbert-lang-8b935a31

Made in the USA
Middletown, DE
23 November 2020